EXPERIMENTING LANDSCAPES

Métis International Garden Festival | Emily Waugh

EXPERIMENTING LANDSCAPES
Testing the Limits of the Garden

Birkhäuser
Basel

Layout, cover design, and typesetting
Vera Pechel, Basel

Project management
Henriette Mueller-Stahl, Berlin

Production
Katja Jaeger, Berlin

Paper
135 g/m² Hello Fat Matt 1.1

Library of Congress Cataloging-in-Publication data
A CIP catalog record for this book has been applied for at the Library of Congress.

Bibliographic information published by the German National Library
The German National Library lists this publication in the Deutsche Nationalbibliografie; detailed bibliographic data are available on the Internet at http://dnb.dnb.de.

This publication is also available as an e-book
(ISBN PDF 978-3-03821-559-2; ISBN EPUB 978-3-03821-577-6).

P.O. Box 44, 4009 Basel, Switzerland
Part of Walter de Gruyter GmbH, Berlin/Boston

Printed on acid-free paper produced from chlorine-free pulp. TCF ∞

Printed in Germany

ISBN 978-3-03821-931-6

9 8 7 6 5 4 3 2 1 www.birkhauser.com

PREFACE

FERTILE TERRAIN

Alexander Reford
Director, Les Jardins de Métis

The gardens and grounds in Métis are fertile terrain for trial and error. These are the exact words that Elsie Reford used when describing her first attempts to create a garden out of a spruce forest in the 1920s.

Now, 90 years later, we have exhibited the work of more than 500 landscape architects, architects, artists, and designers from diverse fields. The wide range of installations is a consequence of the open nature of our competition and the liberty afforded participating designers from around the world. But it is also the result of our express wish to encourage experimentation and offer the conditions to allow for creative new landscapes to take form. The festival was initiated to offer a platform for the exhibition of creative landscapes. Each edition features 20 or more installations, at least five of which are assembled in the eight weeks between the time the snow melts and opening day at the end of June and presented as the new gardens of the current edition. There is no 'featured' garden—no focus on a single installation. Creators, well-known or just discovered, are provided with the same signage and equal visibility. While visitors can identify their favourite piece as they leave, there are no judges and no award for the installation with the greatest number of votes. The only prize is the possibility of being exhibited for another season.

The build schedule is tight, as are the budgets—just 20,000 CAD for materials and labour. This voluntary simplicity reinforces the strength of each concept. There is no excess. There are no extras. Almost all of the materials are sourced locally. There is a lot of borrowing and a little begging. Fabrication is done in our workshops. There are many undeclared hours of work on the part of the designers and by the team, who begin work on May 1 to commence the layout and building. The last week leading up to the opening is a frenzied pulse of machinery and movement. As many as 50 designers and just as many workers and volunteers work side by side to bring the projects to completion in June every year.

Visitors are often sparse on opening day but they swell to more than 1,000 per day in July and August. The warm weather and summer holidays bring families in large numbers. When children emerge from the forested path onto the festival site, they are greeted with installations that occupy every open space. Most of our visitors (more than 5 million since the gardens were opened to the public in 1962) are drawn by the historic gardens and the horticultural displays. The festival and its installations are a bonus—a surprise for some and the key reason for their long trip for others. Contemporary gardens are not to everyone's taste (we have learned over time that the most avid gardeners and talented horticulturists are the most difficult to convert), but children intuitively understand the invitation to action and interaction. They respond to the impulse to climb, to touch, and to explore with an enthusiasm rarely experienced in the more traditional gardens, where visitors are confined to narrow pathways and where hushed murmurs of delight is the common vocabulary. The festival experience is different. It is liberating. It is free. And it is exploratory.

All of the contributors to this book highlight how Métis has offered a platform for their creativity. This is exactly what led us to create the festival. We felt that designers, whether emerging or experienced, needed a venue to create, a place to experiment, and a public to probe and provoke. We felt that we could offer such a venue—a site without restrictions and a curatorial approach that imposed few constraints. We could also provide a public—ready to explore, seeking new experiences, and open to interactivity. We were also driven by a wish to highlight the importance of the garden and landscape generally as a sphere of contemporary creation—as important as the visual arts, film, literature, music, or dance. In the year 2000, this was still an eccentric, even radical position.

No book can do justice to the visual power of these contemporary landscapes or the experiences enjoyed when interacting with them. But we felt the need to document the extraordinary installations we have been privileged to exhibit over the past decade. Giving voice to designers is what we enjoy doing. Seeing their projects come to life in the photographs and drawings on these pages illustrates the ongoing importance of the festival as fertile terrain for experimentation.

INTRODUCTION
TESTING THE LIMITS OF THE GARDEN

Emily Waugh

More than 90 years after Elsie Reford defied convention to grow exotic perennials as far north as the 49th parallel, the designers at the International Garden Festival at Métis continue to test the limits of the garden. Advancing Elsie's legacy of experimentation and what she called 'adventuring' with different soils, plant materials, and hybrid species, the contemporary gardens at the Métis International Garden Festival continue to evolve as a living laboratory for exploration, innovation, and experimentation.

THE GARDEN AS A LANDSCAPE LABORATORY
Any gardener can tell you that, in fact, every garden is a laboratory. Whether a backyard vegetable plot, a sweeping historic estate, or a cluster of containers on a 15th-floor balcony, every time we set out to manipulate the materials of landscape, we are conducting controlled experiments.

These are not random trials, but carefully thought-out procedures to test a hypothesis about soils, exposure, climates, species selection, and so on. Like all experiments, they are rigorous observations of cause and effect: what outcome will occur if a specific factor is manipulated? If I add more acid to this soil, will my rhododendrons thrive? If I plant ferns from a higher hardiness zone, will they survive the winter in pots? If I plant native wildflowers, can I protect the shrinking population of crucial pollinator bees and insects? Through these calculated trials and resulting adaptations and innovations, gardeners are always testing the capacity of their site conditions, their climates, and their own knowledge and skills as gardeners.

A NEW HYPOTHESIS FOR A NEW KIND OF GARDEN
When the right questions are asked, these experiments can transform how we make gardens, how we expect gardens to perform, what we understand gardens to be, and, in some cases, how we understand the world around us.

In Ancient Egypt, the prosperous New Kingdom transformed the garden from agricultural-scale food production to ornamental pleasure grounds by asking, "Can we channel the floodwaters of the Nile for irrigation to sustain our own personal paradises?"[1]

In the 18th century Princess Augusta dared to ask, "Is it possible for Kew Gardens to contain all the plants known on Earth?" This ambitious pursuit (taken up by Augusta's son King George III) shifted the gardens at Kew from a collection of fol-

[1] *Landscape Design Online: Ancient Egypt*, website accessed on 13 April 2016.

lies to, not only the leading botanical garden in the world, but a critical resource for expanding the British Empire.[2]

In the 1950s, landscape architect Garrett Eckbo rebelled against his Beaux Arts training and began to define modern landscape architecture by posing a different hypothesis: What if we fit design to the needs and desires of contemporary life? His reoccurring mantra, "Gardens are places in which people live out of doors", altered expectations for how gardens and landscapes could perform and how designers could include function, not just aesthetics in landscape design.[3]

Our understanding of landscape architecture and the garden changed again in the late 1970s when young landscape architect Martha Schwartz constructed a front-yard garden using bagels and purple aquarium gravel. When the 'Bagel Garden' appeared on the cover of *Landscape Architecture Magazine*, many readers were so offended that this work could be recognized by the profession that they cancelled their subscriptions on the spot. But this marriage of art and landscape forever changed the practice of landscape architecture.

In contemporary gardens, the incorporation of technology (both physical and digital) has allowed designers to further explore the physical potential of the built landscape. We see this in the vertical gardens of Patrick Blanc (based on the 'botanical brick' introduced by Stanley H. White in 1938) which challenged and subsequently changed our expectations of what a garden could look like and what conditions are necessary for plant material to grow. The 3 and even 4-dimensional modeling technology used by design offices today, has further advanced the formal and technical capabilities of the designed landscape. In every case, gardeners, designers, and landscape architects are continually reconsidering the hypothesis to push the limits of the garden.

THE GARDEN FESTIVAL AS A VENUE FOR BREAKING DOWN BARRIERS

Outside of the constraints of professional landscape architecture and garden design practice, contemporary garden festivals offer a laboratory venue to designers around the world. These annual exhibitions (notably, Festival International des Jardins de Chaumont-sur-Loire, France, the Cornerstone Festival in Sonoma, California, USA, The Chelsea Fringe in London, UK, and the International Garden Festival at Métis, Canada) have spread in ambition and scope to create a hybrid of gardens, art, landscape, technology, and design that continually

[2] *Cruickshank on Kew: The Garden That Changed the World*, BBC TV programme of 28 April 2009.

[3] Treib, Marc, and Dorothée Imbert. *Garrett Eckbo: Modern Landscapes for Living.* Berkeley: University of California Press, 1997.

challenges our understanding of the garden and what it can be. Each of these venues offers a different expression of gardens, landscape, and art, but each has at its core an idea of experimentation.

The gardens at these festivals attempt to expand the boundaries of the discipline itself as they break down, blend, and rebuild the borders of traditional gardens, contemporary landscape architecture, architecture, and contemporary art. Their scales and sometimes their materials reflect traditional gardening. Their scope, methods, and conceptual basis more closely resemble contemporary landscape and architecture, and their desire to provoke and challenge is aligned with contemporary art.

Each festival has its own character, its own design sensibility, and its own approach to experimentation defined in part by its founding ethos, history, physical layout, context, and attitude toward the garden.

THE SPIRIT OF MÉTIS

At Métis there is a powerful and legible influence from a curiously consistent list of factors that we have identified through interviews with designers, expert essays, and the installations themselves. Every festival participant we spoke to during this process was able to articulate some combination of the same factors that allowed them to experiment freely at Métis: the constant presence of Elsie Reford's pioneering spirit; the temporary nature of the installations which frees designers from the constraints of durability and performance expectations; the rugged, remote, and somewhat forebidding landscape that stirs a curiosity and almost demands a different design approach; the fact that designers must install their own work, forcing experimentation with materials and methods; and the open support of festival director, Alexander Reford, for complete creative freedom. At Métis the entire process is open. The competition for entry is an open call to designers and artists across disciplines, the jury is open to all ideas (unlike in professional practice, at Métis there is no brief), and the design and construction is open to anything the designers propose. The only limits are time, budget, and the (seemingly limitless) creative capacity of the designers.

Finally, with every experiment, there is a possibility of failure. Unlike professional practice, where failure is unacceptable—landscapes must perform to a certain specification, codes must be respected, client needs must be met—the possibility of failure is almost written into the process at Métis, giving designers permission to truly experiment.

A LEGACY OF ADVENTURING

When Elsie Reford first began gardening in 1926 (after appendicitis surgery at age 54 required her to give up fishing and slow down), she faced a number of obstacles that most other gardeners would have seen as limiting. She had no formal training and no professional design help. She faced severe allergies that often left her bed-ridden, a seemingly inhospitable climate, and a site that was selected first as a fishing lodge with no consideration for gardening conditions (climate, soil quality, or protection from the winds of the St. Lawrence River).[4] The greatest obstacle—and the one that Elsie Reford is most famous for overcoming—was geography. How could anyone possibly propagate rare exotic perennials so close to the 49th parallel?

With no exact references or examples to turn to, Elsie was forced to experiment, to establish her own methods, materials, and approach. Over time, Elsie became an expert plants woman—adapting conditions to meet the needs of each species she wished to establish and ultimately changing perceptions of what kind of garden could be achieved in these Nordic conditions.

THE POTENTIAL OF THE GARDEN TO ALTER PERCEPTION

The festival gardens at Métis are both an extension of and a departure from Elsie Reford's traditional gardens. They continue her rigorous experimentation, trial and error, and 'why not try?' attitude, but instead of experimenting with horticultural material, they are experimenting with the nature of the garden itself.

The gardens in the earlier years of the festival (represented in Lesley Johnstone's *Hybrids: Reshaping the Contemporary Gardens in Métis*, 2007) boldly challenge the limits of what a garden can be, asking questions such as, "What on earth is a garden?", "Is it still a garden if it doesn't have any plants?", "Is a garden simply an enclosure or can it also be a fragment of the greater landscape beyond?"

The collection of gardens featured in *Experimenting Landscapes*—primarily, but not exclusively, from the 2008–2015 festival editions—shift the experiment from testing the limit of what a garden can be, to testing the limit of what a garden can do. And more specifically, what is the potential of the garden to change our perception of the world around us? These designers use the medium of the garden to open our eyes (and other senses) to heighten our awareness of the phenomena, processes, relationships, materials, and landscapes that we often can't see, that we overlook, or that we have seen so often that we have simply forgotten to look.

Each of these gardens asks, if we slightly alter the composition, the viewpoint, the structure, the materials, or the experience of the landscape, can we change how people see even the most familiar things? How they understand them? How they engage with them? How they value them? Some of these gardens offer us a clear, in-depth understanding of something that we would otherwise not be able to see because it is hidden by complexity or scale. Some simply focus our attention on something to help us see it differently, or in some cases to help us see it at all. Others offer us new vantage points to see even the most familiar things in a new way. Some change our perception of function, value, and meaning by challenging our expectations of everyday things. And some offer us a completely new awareness of the landscape simply by allowing us to experience it.

[4] Reford, Alexander. *The Reford Gardens: Elsie's Paradise.* Montréal: Les Éditions de L'Homme, 2004.

MATERIALS AND METHODS

Each garden is presented through photographs and drawings, quotations extracted from designer interviews, and a brief project description modeled after a scientific experiment report: abstract, method, result, and materials. Through five different methods (and corresponding chapter titles: *Disaggregate and Re-Present*, *Focus within Frames*, *Altered Viewpoints*, *Unexpected Materials and Contexts*, *Landscape as a Living Experience*) these gardens invite closer readings of the landscape, offering us new perspectives.

The three essays in the book complement the investigation of the Métis International Garden Festival as a landscape laboratory: the particular conditions here that allow for experimentation, how it is different than other festivals, and the relationship between the festival and contemporary landscape practice.

Although a printed book can never reproduce the visual, sensory, and experiential quality of a visit through these gardens, we hope that through these words and images, we can invite a closer reading of the Métis environment, to sharpen your focus on the landscapes and phenomena explored in the gardens, and maybe even begin to alter your perception of the world around you.

Elsie Reford in her garden

GROUNDS FOR EXPERIMENTATION

REFLECTIONS ON MÉTIS AS A LANDSCAPE LABORATORY

ELSIE'S EXPERIMENTS

Alexander Reford
Director, Les Jardins de Métis,
and great-grandson of Elsie Reford

"Elsie Reford had more of a botanical or collector's garden approach, which is a bit of an exception in the gardening world. Most people garden because it brings them pleasure and happiness and beauty, but Elsie was amassing collections with some systematic consistency. She wanted, for instance, every species of lilies that can be grown.

In that era—she began the garden in 1926—there was not a lot of printed material and there were not a lot of examples to follow in Canada so she would look at an English garden and say, 'Well, if they can grow it in Dorset then I can grow it here. Why not try?'

There was a wonderful moment each spring where Elsie went back to her garden to deal with the disaster, but also regale herself with her success because the plants had come back to life. She was working with plants regarding which most people would have told her (and did), 'What's the point? It's not going to work. Too cold. Winters are too long'. People simply didn't know if some of these plants would survive the winter and when they did she was proud. If they didn't, she would move the plant to a new venue, or try a variant of that plant. She would give herself the time to try again. There are a couple of cases where she tried it here, she tried it there, she tried it in a third place. And by the fourth or fifth effort she was successful.

In 1926 when Elsie started, her plant selection list was pretty easy and not too interesting, but by 1930 it was more sophisticated. By 1935 she was collecting plants that were relatively unheard of in North America and by 1940 she was dealing with an even more advanced selection of unusual plants. There was nobody else doing it in a climate of that kind, so with nobody to compare herself to, she could only be constrained by her own lack of imagination.

Elsie didn't work from a drawing or a master plan, so the garden was never finished. There was always a new component that she was working on—it was never stopped in time. She never said, 'I'm so happy with my garden I'm just going to sit down in my chaise longue and enjoy it'. It's that perverse reality that people are never really satisfied with what they've created. With the festival, that's one of the things that impels us to keep doing these competitions and giving ourselves all this work as opposed to just curating this as a permanent or finished composition. We have this need to progress and that's something she had as well."

A DIFFERENT APPROACH

Chris Reed

Stoss Landscape Urbanism

Safe Zone, 2006–2009

"Garden festivals, and specifically Métis, give landscape architects an equivalent to a gallery installation, which is something that has always been available to architects, but isn't always conducive to the kinds of things we are taking on—the scale, the materiality, the living nature of landscape.

But, at Métis, you're out in the environment, much like most of our work. And while there is a public that comes through, it is in a different kind of setting than a public park or open space. People are there because they understand the cultural ambition of the place, they are as much there to learn, and explore, and play as they are to engage on a more intellectual level with the kinds of experiments that are being put into play.

The starting point at Métis, of course, is the beautiful traditional gardens, but now the festival has added a completely different dimension to it. It's almost as if they have taken over the back lot and said, 'We're out of the *proper* garden, now it's time to get dirty and experiment and play and be a little bit devious and mischievous about what we can do'. If the historic gardens are the garden of the past, the question becomes, 'What is the garden of the future?', or ,'What are the many gardens of the future?' They have established quite clearly grounds for experimentation.

It's a different way to approach landscape. Landscape as event. Landscape as a sequence of curated spaces that are constantly changing over a number of years. Traditional gardens might change seasonally, or with events happening within them, but here the entire garden is reformulated every few years. This is really at the core of what this place is about. There are very few permanent elements—some pathways and basic site delineations—but beyond that everything is in a constant state of change.

Its remoteness also gives it a special quality. It is so far out of the way that the people who go there are going there for a reason. It's part of their journey. You're not quite sure what you are going to see at the end of that journey because of the way it changes. You might like it, you might not, but you know it's going to be something pretty interesting."

Aerial view of festival site

Le Jardin des Hespérides, CAO PERROT

THE SPIRIT OF MÉTIS
Andy Cao and Xavier Perrot
CAO PERROT

Le Jardin des Hespérides, 2006–2007

"There are really three parameters that we think about at Métis. One is the site itself. Métis is just so different from every other site we've been to. It's different from Chaumont, or Cornerstone. You feel alive when you're there. Being by the St. Lawrence is almost like being by the sea—the air is salty, but you are in the woods, the light is different, the people—you have all of these notes that really inspire the projects.

The second is the total creative freedom to come up with something new. Designers tend to get comfortable after time, and unintentionally get a signature style or approach. To get away from that, we have to keep exploring something new for ourselves. For us, Métis was the first time that we explored a place for dreaming, where it's not about telling a story, not about narrative, but about the whole immersive environment. A place where you can slow down, and experience, and discover. All of these elements started showing up in one way or another in different forms in our work. This creative freedom gave us this possibility to make a big jump to a new era as designers.

And the third is the historical spirit of the place. Elsie Reford was also experimenting with plants, so we asked ourselves, 'How do we continue experimenting? How do we carry on this idea of trying things?' Being in that environment, you start seeing things differently. There's lots of room for improvization, lots of room for being spontaneous, for trial and error, and not being afraid of failure. It is not just about doing research or gathering data about a material and then choosing a material from your material library—here on site, when it is hands-on, you have to be there working with it, figuring out what works and what doesn't work. We have to be there to do the work. To figure it out. You have to go there and completely immerse yourself in the making. You really get a different insight than you would, say, experimenting with something in your studio. For us that is so valuable.

It's in keeping with the spirit of the Reford Gardens, the idea of 'just keep trying'. It's about having an idea and figuring out how it can be realized and what you take away from it. That's what is so special about Métis, that kind of adventurous spirit. You just keep trying."

LEARNING ON THE GROUND

Alissa North
North Design Office

Core Sample, 2006–2008

"The Métis Festival gives small practices the opportunity to realize a vision at a small scale. The idea starts conceptually, but then it has to be transformed into materials and space. You have to specify all the materials, design the details, and build it with your own hands.

What's different about Métis is that you can't just go to a standard detail book, you have to go through the process of imagining and designing your own details from scratch. We did a lot of research before building Core Sample, testing materials and building mock-ups in our backyard to make sure it was going to work. We spent a lot of time figuring out what liquid we could use inside the tubes that would last over winter, that wouldn't freeze, that wouldn't discolour everything, and so on.

Then, of course, you get there and the construction team might tell you it's not possible to install it exactly the way you had planned because of the particular site conditions—geological conditions, seasonal conditions, tree roots—that force you to adjust and compromise. There is an experienced crew there to help you, but you are ultimately left to your own devices to work it out—it's really important for designers to get that experience.

For that reason, we are always trying to find these kinds of opportunities for our students. A lot of them come to graduate school and don't have that hands-on experience, for example, how do two materials attach? Many of them have office experience, but it's different than the process of designing something, and having to work it, and re-work it because you have to build it with your own hands. That kind of hands-on experience is really important to the discipline.

Alexander Reford is a big part of fostering that experience—he is open to anything. Maybe it's a Reford characteristic to want to experiment. You give something a try and if the project fails, it fails. The festival really provides young designers with an opportunity to do something innovative, a place to push ideas."

University of Toronto students install *Macro/Micro/Myco*, 2015.

P.S. 19, Queens, New York

POSITIVE TRANSFORMATIONS

Ken Smith

A Ditch With A View, 2011–

"In our office, installations like the garden we did at Métis are an R+D methodology for developing new things that may or may not end up in the bigger and more permanent projects. They are definitely not less work. If you look at them rationally on a time and material basis, they don't make any sense at all, but the temporariness of installations allows for a much more experimental proposition, which is why we have always liked doing them. They allow us to explore new materials and fabrication techniques because you can work with less durable materials and you can put them together on the fly because they don't need to last forever.

We experiment with forms and ideas that get re-used. Sometimes we find out that something we planned to do on the cheap actually turns out to be a good method and is worth using again. An example is the Glowing Topiary Garden in New York, which we constructed using awning frames and backlit vinyl. I didn't anticipate that we would use vinyl again, but in fact, we have.

Installations are also a quick and inexpensive way to make positive transformations in the kinds of spaces that contemporary landscape architects are now dealing with. A lot of times we don't actually register urban infrastructure, or interstitial spaces—we see them as just a background of the city. Installations might cause people to actually see them and even look at them differently, and think about them, and maybe change people's opinion of what is beautiful or not, or what is valuable or not, or what is interesting or not.

P.S. 19 in Queens, New York, was an interesting project in that way. It had a 12-foot-tall rusty chain-link fence around it and it was all asphalt. We stretched a scrim across the top half of the fence that was printed with blue sky and clouds, and using traffic paint we did some very simple super graphics on the asphalt playground. The scrim and the painted asphalt transformed something that was pretty urban and tough into something that was actually fun. Not really fundamentally different, but it made a really positive transformation of the schoolyard, the kids and the parents all loved it. It happened very fast and it was cheap. Again, it was the vinyl we had discovered for the topiary garden."

BEYOND THE GARDENS

Paula Meijerink

SE BUSCA / WANTED Landscape

Asphalt Garden, 2003

"There are three pieces that play a role in the capacity of the larger landscape laboratory. There are the historical gardens, the gardens in the festival, and the larger landscape around the festival site—the St. Lawrence River, the shoreline, flooding, erosion protection, infrastructure, cultural interpretation, and so on. For the gardens to address these issues on and around their property, it's really pushing forward the limits of landscape architecture.

For example, since the 2010 flood damaged more than 40 properties along the shoreline, the gardens' landscape laboratory has been studying other properties along the river that are precariously close to the water and could possibly be destroyed with the next great storm. So, what happens with zoning, what happens with the people who live there, with their property? And how can this become a positive rather than a precarious condition?

A lot of this work can be done with students as well. When I was at the Université de Montréal, we did a studio with third-year landscape architecture students that focused on preserving a culturally important bridge over the Mitis River where it enters the St. Lawrence. It is the bridge you cross as you enter the gardens and it is to be replaced with a newer one about 50 metres up the river. The question was, 'How can this bridge be a community centre for the region and for tourists coming to the region?' It deals with the floodplain, it deals with the St. Lawrence River, it deals with infrastructure, and it deals with multiple regional questions. It gives you an idea of how a project that is slightly outside the boundaries of the festival can have other impacts. If the gardens weren't there, this project would not be happening. Everything starts with the garden.

The gardens are a breeding ground for new ideas and the value of those gardens goes beyond the limits of the site. They become precedents for bigger, global projects. People see the gardens here and in publications, and are inspired to do other projects similar to them. They say, 'Hey, we can do roly-poly rubber because it's already been done there!' They show the never-ending possibilities for landscape architecture and that the potential of landscape is infinitely rich."

Université de Montréal students visit the bridge over the Mitis River, 2014.

Festival director Alexander Reford (right) discusses climate change in Québec with documentary photographer Joan Sullivan.

DISAGGREGATE AND RE-PRESENT

We use the expression 'Cannot see the forest for the trees' to describe someone who is so focused on individual elements or details that they fail to see how they come together to form a whole. The gardens in this chapter address the opposite condition—when we look only at the aggregate or the whole system and fail to see the beauty or meaning in its component parts. Instead of asking us to step back to take in a larger view, these gardens ask us to step in and focus our attention on the compositional elements that make up a particular landscape, region, or eco-system.

The designers re-focus our attention on these smaller elements by disaggregating larger systems into their component parts and then re-presenting them in isolation. By removing these often-overlooked elements from their original contexts, these gardens offer us a more in-depth understanding of something that we would otherwise not be able to see because of the complexity, scale, or density of the original system.

In some of these gardens (*Tiny Taxonomy*, *Core Sample*, *La collection du jardinier*), the materials are physically removed and collected from the local environment and re-presented as singular elements to highlight them and focus our attention on the parts themselves. The others (*Floating Forest*, *Every Garden Needs a Shed and a Lawn!*) more abstractly dissect the concept of the whole to make us reconsider the larger system itself.

By highlighting the individual components of these larger systems in an ordered schema, these gardens give us a different understanding of both the elements and the whole itself, allowing us to see both the forest and the trees.

TINY TAXONOMY
Rosetta Elkin

2010–

Abstract

Tiny Taxonomy isolates the often-overlooked plants of the forest floor and presents them as a taxonomy—a classified system that recasts these smallest of species as working components of the natural environment.

Method

The taxonomy is displayed in 42 constructed habitats designed to be seen as extrusions of the forest floor, each presenting one plant species for closer consideration. The habitats—a grid of mirrored cylinders ranging in height from 30 to 150 centimetres —bring each plant to eye level, allowing a zoomed-in connection with these most fragile and tiny plants.

When these plants—individually foraged from a distant corner of a local property—are removed from their natural environments where they are tangled up as they compete for resources, we are able to reflect on and admire their individual forms.

Although each species is exhibited in isolation, the reflective surface of the cylindrical structures re-contextualizes the plants within the surrounding forest, allowing visitors to reconnect these 'tiny operators' with their natural habitats.

Result

This display of foraged boreal forest natives pushes us to slow down and take a closer look at plant material, not just as commercially available species that we see potted in nurseries, but as small players in a much larger forest system.

Materials

42 mirrored cylinders, selection of locally foraged forest floor plants selected to re-present surrounding forest conditions

The tiny plants of the forest floor are displayed in 42 constructed habitats.

Cowslip (*primula florindae*)

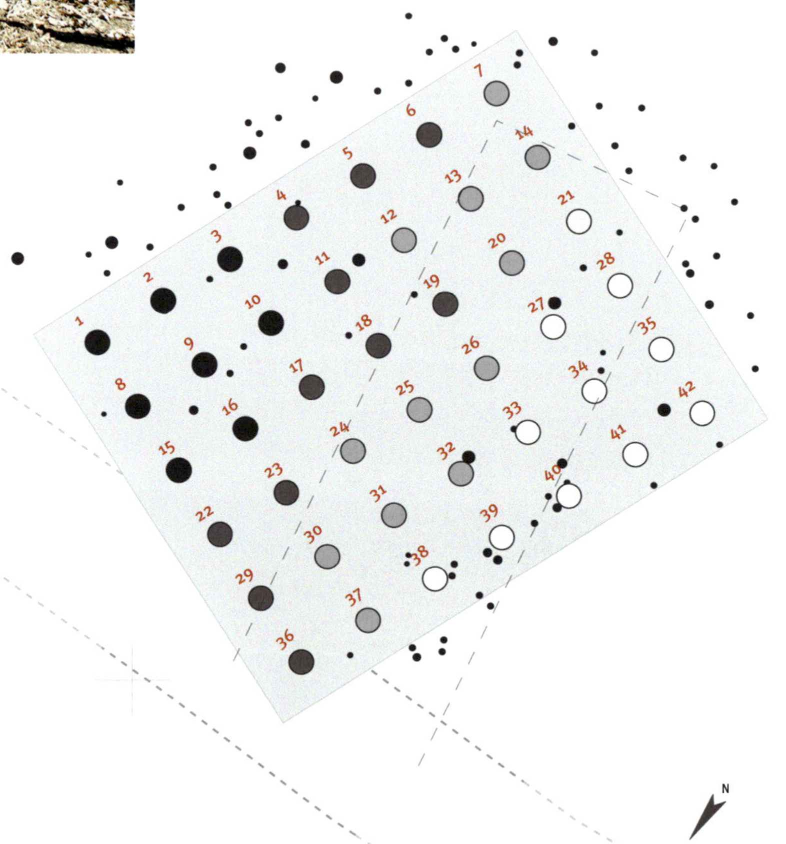

1 Northern blueberry *(vaccinium boreale)*
2 Lady fern *(athyrium filix-femina)*
3 Alpine bearberry *(arctostaphylos alpine)*
Alpine violet *(viola labradorica)*
4 Solomon's seal *(polygonatum biflorum)*
5 Canada mayflower *(maianthemum canadense)*
6 Beech fern *(dryopteris phegopteris)*
7 Wood forget-me-not *(myosotis sylvatica)*
8 Dwarf windflower *(anenome multifida 'Rubra')*
9 White spruce *(picea glauca)*
10 Dwarf iris *(iris pumilla)*
11 Lily of the valley *(convallaria majalis)*
12 Azure bluet *(houstonia caerulea)*
13 Siberian squil *(scilla siberica)*, pearlwort *(sagina subulata)*
14 Spiked sedge *(carex spicata)*
15 Blue-eyed grass *(sisyrinchium angustifolium)*
16 Sandwort *(arenaria hookeri)*
17 Cowslip *(primula florindae)*
18 Lingonberry *(vaccinium vitis-idaea)*
19 Dwarf astilbe *(astilbe chinensis 'Pumila')*
20 Yellow barrenwort *(epimedium versicolor 'Sulphureum')*
21 Mountain phlox *(phlox subulata 'Rose')*
22 Pink lady's slipper *(cypripedium acaule)*
23 Candelabra primrose *(primula bulleesiana)*
24 Bunchberry *(comus canadensis)*
25 Barren strawberry *(waldsteinia fragarioides)*
26 Tatting fern *(athyrium filix-femina 'Frizelliae')*
27 Fairy spuds *(claytonia virginica)*
28 Edelweiss *(leontopodium alpinus)*
29 Maiden pink *(dianthus delt. 'Flashing Light')*
30 Plumbago *(ceratostigma plumbaginoides)*
31 Common oak sedge *(carex pensylvanica)*
32 Alpine aster *(aster alpinus 'Albus')*
33 Poker primrose *(primula sikkimensis)*
34 Devil's paintbrush *(pilosella aurantiaca)*
35 Dwarf goat's beard *(aruncus aethusifolius)*
36 Sea thrift *(armeria maritima 'Laucheana')*
37 Fan columbine *(aquilegia flabellata 'Ministar')*
38 Pink-flowering strawberry *(fragaria x. 'Shades of Pink')*
39 Fairy thimble bellflower *(campanula cochlearifolia)*
40 Western mugwort *(artemisia ludoviciana)*
41 Marsh marigold *(caltha palustris)*
42 Livelong saxifrage *(saxifraga paniculata)*

White spruce (*picea glauca*)

"It's rare to see something as multifarious as a forest broken down into parts. We think of taking apart a car engine to see how it works, but rarely do we treat the natural world as having parts."

Rosetta Elkin

Broom moss (*dicranales*)

Pink lady's slipper orchid (*cypripedium acaule*)

CORE SAMPLE
North Design Office
2006–2008

Abstract
Drawing from the model of the core sample—which extracts material from a site to understand its geological composition—*Core Sample* highlights the detailed landscape textures that are often overshadowed by the dominant forces of Québec's Gaspé Peninsula region: the river, the mountains, and the ever-present winds.

Method
In a nod to Elsie Reford's tradition of collecting, sampling and propagating to better understand the micro-conditions of her garden site, North Design Office mined the local landscape for a range of textures and materials including seeds, shells, stones, and found objects, and displayed them in a grid of transparent columns, each containing a different solitary element. The flowing topography of the site—grassy landforms that appear boundless and shifting—alludes to the landscape of the Gaspé region: the hills to the south of the festival site and the rocky islands in the seaway to the north. Planted with a variety of tall grasses (rye, barley, oats, and triticale), the mounds add dynamic movement to the site, as the grasses catch and respond to the wind.

Result
By isolating these textures and then re-presenting them within a topography that recalls the larger Gaspé landscape, the garden simultaneously focuses our attention on the beauty of the micro-scale elements of the site and the complex macro-scale composition of the region.

Materials
Locally collected landscape elements such as seeds, shells, stones, and a variety of plants; 107 2.4 metre acrylic tubes; earth mounds covered with local grasses such as rye, barley, oats, and triticale

107 acrylic tubes each display one material collected from the local landscape.

“It’s the shifting of scale that brings more of an acute awareness to the site. There is magic in these smaller moments.”

Peter North, North Design Office

Flowing landforms reflect the topography of the Gaspé region.

LA COLLECTION DU JARDINIER
Les attentives
2012–2014

Abstract
La collection du jardinier focuses our attention on the often overlooked beauty of the 'un-gardened' plant material on the Métis site—spontaneous vegetation, indigenous plants, and the discarded waste material from Elsie Reford's gardens.

Method
In contrast to Elsie Reford's process of rigorous control in her garden, *La collection du jardinier* highlights the beauty of the clippings, deadheads, and fallen blossoms collected daily from the gardener's compost bins. The material is sorted, dissected, re-arranged, and presented as small sculptures that offer visitors an intimate and detailed look at the plants we see in the gardens.

The installation leads visitors along a discovery trail through three venues, each offering a different relationship to the plant material: the working garden shed in the historic gardens, where the designers sort and prepare the plants and blossoms; the photographer's dark room in Estevan Lodge, where visitors can have an intimate sensory experience with large quantities of plant material deposited in the large developer's sink; and a small greenhouse in a field on the festival site, where visitors continue their detailed observation, this time in the original un-gardened landscape.

Result
The installation asks visitors to enter a different 'time zone' and, instead of moving quickly past things without much notice, to slow down and to sharpen their focus on the details of the individual plants that make up the formal gardens—the patterns, the variation of forms, the colours, the smells, the delicacy, the cycles of growth and decay, and life's infinite particularities.

Materials
Waste material, cuttings, and deadheads collected daily from Elsie Reford's gardens

Plant material is sorted, prepared, and displayed in the garden shed at the historic gardens.

The collection extends to a small greenhouse on the festival site.

"It's a magnifying moment when you are looking at little parts of things, and taking in something very detailed. This takes a different kind of time."

Chloé Fortin

Large quantities of recovered garden waste are presented in the darkroom at Estevan Lodge.

FLOATING FOREST

NIPpaysage

2012

Abstract

Floating Forest, an offsite installation presented by the Métis International Garden Festival at Chelsea Fringe, conceptually and literally dismantles a section of forest from Québec, Canada, and re-presents it in London, England, revealing the connection between the province's forestry industry and the construction of many of London's 19th-century buildings. These structures were built using enormous white pine trees that were felled along Québec's river valleys, squared, floated, and then shipped across the Atlantic.

Method

This seemingly simple grid of 450 red cedar rounds (used to represent the historic white pines) tell a multi-layered story of this complex relationship. The forest itself is seen in the choice of materials; the logging industry is present in both the processed timber rounds and in the characteristic grid layout of post-logging reforestation; the local and transatlantic transportation of material are seen in the floating logs as well as in the physical location of the wood nearly 5,000 kilometres from its origin; and the end use of this material is revealed in the composition of the surrounding historic wharf buildings on the Portobello dock section of the Grand Union Canal near West London's Ladbroke Grove. The rounds measure between 30 and 40 centimetres in diameter and are fixed in a rigorous orthogonal grid with a string attached to a metal grid.

Result

The floating landscape of timber rounds temporarily transforms a small section of the 220-kilometre Grand Union Canal and presents a living history of the link between Québec's forestry industry and the construction of 19th-century London.

Materials

450 cut red cedar rounds and metal strings

A grid of 450 floating timbers transform the Portobello Dock section of London's Grand Union Canal.

The grid pattern shifts slightly with the wind and movement on the canal.

"We like to find a simple and strong way to make one gesture that can be read in multiple ways."

Mélanie Mignault, NIPpaysage

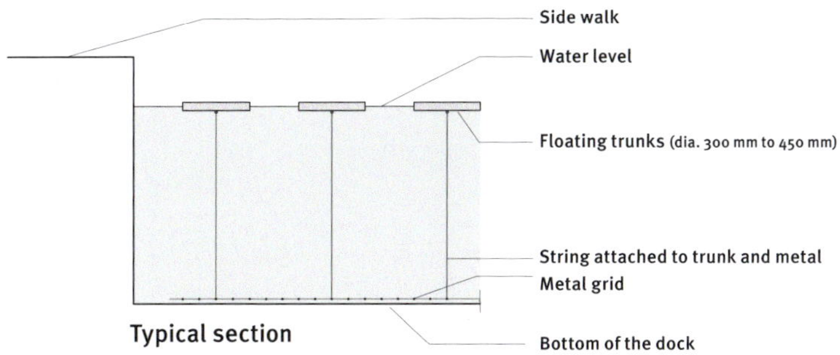

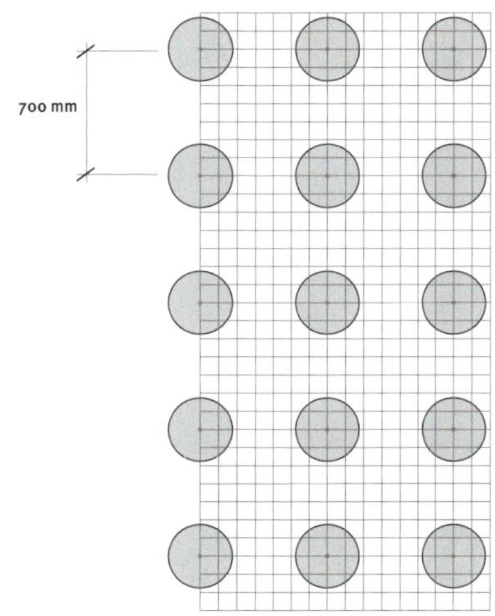

Floating rounds are attached with string to a 70 centimetres metal grid.

Cedar rounds measure between 30 and 40 centimetres in diameter.

EVERY GARDEN NEEDS A SHED AND A LAWN!

Deborah Nagan

2009–2013

Abstract

Every Garden Needs a Shed and a Lawn!—designed as a tenth birthday present to the Métis Festival—identifies the essential elements of garden design. The installation asks visitors to consider the hidden individual layers that form a garden.

Method

Each of the ten essential garden themes—water, seeds, soil, clouds, carbon, pollination, concept, light, food, and beauty—is presented conceptually in the interior of one shed and in a corresponding garden plot outside. In one shed, visitors find shelves lined with canned tomatoes and then look outside to discover a bed of tomato plants. Together, these represent food production in the garden. In another, soil is represented in a shed stacked to the ceiling with bags of garden compost and a garden strewn with local boulders. In another, remnants of Claude Cormier's iconic *Blue Stick Garden* (an abstract reproduction of the traditional Victorian mixed border using painted blue sticks) spill out the door introducing the element of 'concept' in gardening.

Visitors conduct their own investigations through this deconstructed garden, curiously opening shed doors to reveal clues about the next element and how it will be manifest in the corresponding garden.

Result

By selecting and presenting these ten garden components individually, this project compels visitors to address their own ideas about the garden and asks them to consider: Are these the ten elements they would have selected? How would they re-organize them into their own personal paradise gardens?

Materials

Ten painted garden sheds, garden compost, boulders, canned tomatoes, tomato plants, blue sticks, empty pots of blue paint, sculptor's materials and tools, statues, pots of honey, sunflowers, lightbulbs, glass shards, garden hoses, water, band saw blades, stacked logs, glass bottles of seawater, local rocks and ferns, seed packets, corn, table, chairs, and drawing implements

Each of the ten essential garden themes is presented conceptually in the interior of one shed and in a corresponding garden plot outside.

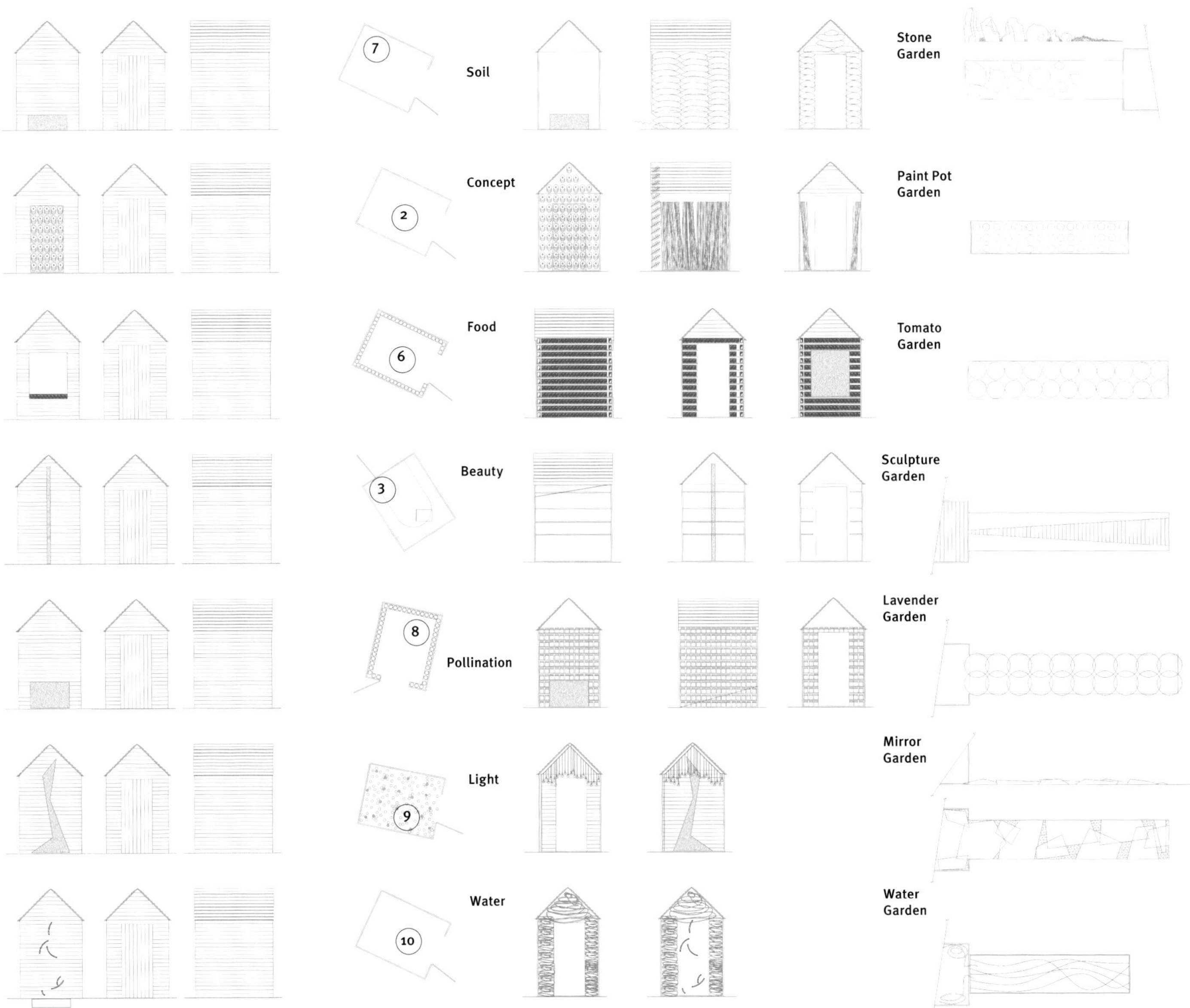

Layouts and specifications for sheds and gardens

"The things that might be obvious to a designer as elements of a garden, are not necessarily going to be obvious to the garden visitor."

Deborah Nagan

Elsie Reford's original table and chair are equipped with drawing paper and pencils to invite visitors to contribute their own ideas to the garden.

Remnants of Claude Cormier's *Blue Stick Garden* represent concept in gardening.

Jars of sea water represent the role of clouds and cloud mist in the garden.

FOCUS WITHIN FRAMES

By placing something within a frame—a photograph, a landscape through binoculars, a still image from a film—we define a field and create a focused view. Sometimes simply by drawing our attention to something, a frame can help us see it differently, change our understanding of its importance, and re-cast our impression of its meaning.

The installations in this chapter use simple frames to focus our attention on something that we otherwise might not have noticed or have seen so many times, that we have forgotten to look. In all of these gardens, the landscape itself is the exhibition, and the designed pieces or frames are simply devices to help us to see that landscape.

By drawing borders around a particular aspect of the Métis site these projects offer us new perspectives, a heightened understanding of the relationship between different elements, and a renewed sense of awe in the simplest things.

Some of the projects in this chapter construct vertical frames in the landscape to guide our view (*A Ditch With A View*), others enclose a three dimensional space that changes not only how we see the site, but also how we occupy it (*Courtesy of Nature*, *Edge Effect*), and others use frames as optical devices to explore our visual perception of the environment around us (*Making Circles in the Water*, *Réflexions colorées*).

By focusing our attention on the particular elements of the natural landscape, these gardens force us to take the time to consider these elements again.

A DITCH WITH A VIEW
Ken Smith

2011–

Abstract
A Ditch With A View uses a series of frames to recast the beauty of a humble piece of infrastructure—a drainage ditch.

Method
Three vertical frames span the width of the ditch, providing windowed views of the ditch itself and the borrowed landscape of the St. Lawrence River beyond. The large frames—constructed from winter-fallen spruce trunks and filled with window sashes recycled from a local monastery—force us first to take notice of the ditch and then to reconsider its real beauty. Through the frames we see the ditch as part of the St. Lawrence landscape, we see the beauty of its spontaneous vegetation, its fluctuating water levels, and the efficiency of its functional form. We also begin to see the ditch as a garden as the 23-metre spaces between the frames become secret garden spaces.

To reflect the scale shift between the small ditch and the almost sea-like river in the distance, the frames progress in height as they move toward the river from 2.5 up to 5 metres.

The monochromatic bluish-grey tones of the installation resonate with the dominant blue/grey palette of the historic gardens, the Gaspé skies, and the rocky St. Lawrence landscape.

Result
Providing a windowed view of the ditch with the dramatic backdrop of the St. Lawrence River takes a space that is not typically considered beautiful and reframes our perception of a typical utilitarian infrastructure.

Materials
Fallen spruce trunks; 122 different-sized window sashes from local salvage yard (56 x 112 centimetres, 66 x 96.5 centimetres, 35.5 x 84 centimetres, 40.5 x 76 centimetres)

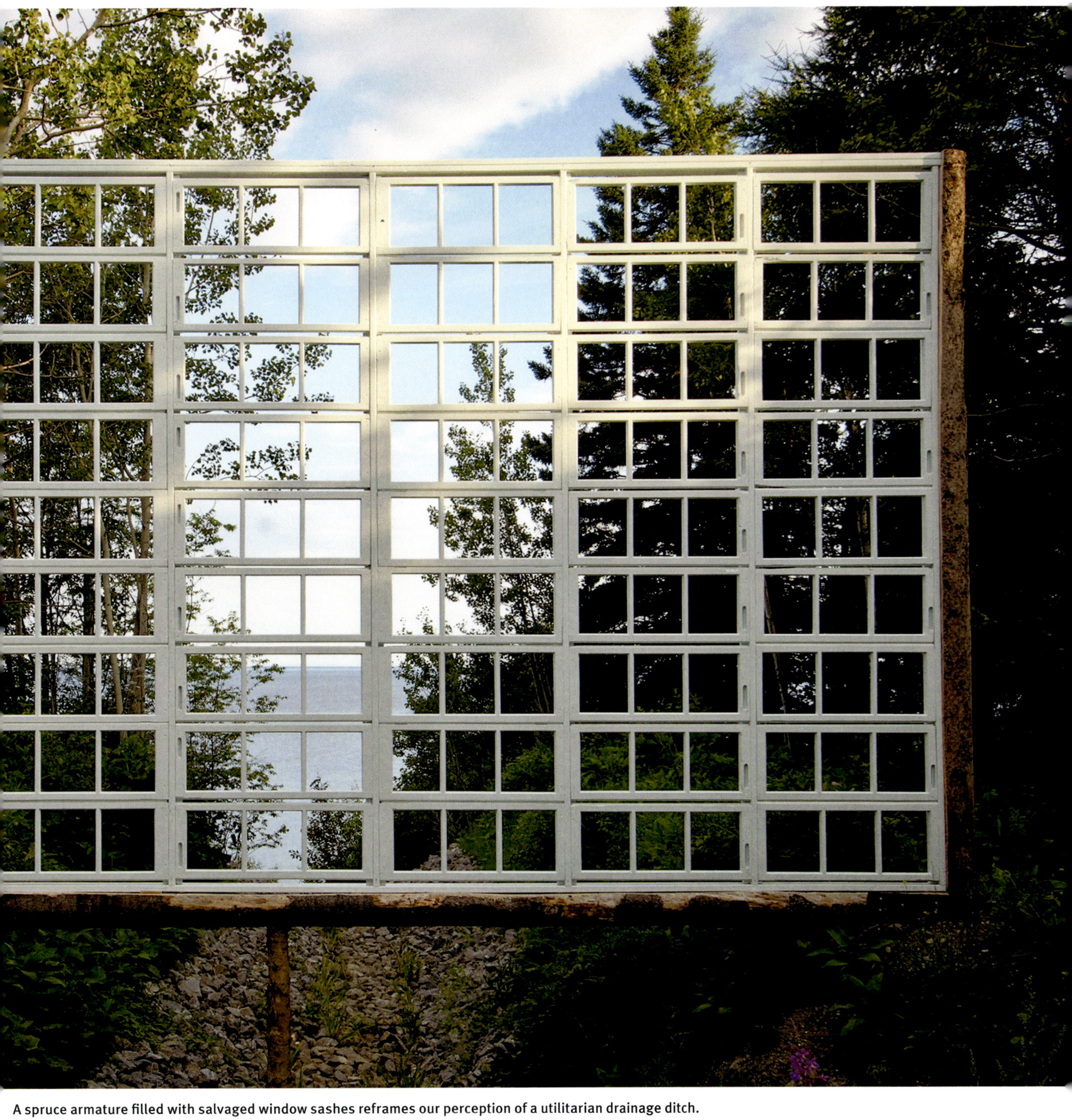

A spruce armature filled with salvaged window sashes reframes our perception of a utilitarian drainage ditch.

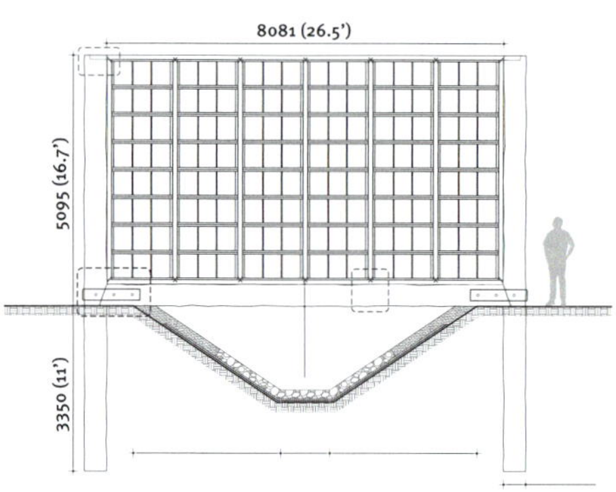

(1) Window frame type 1

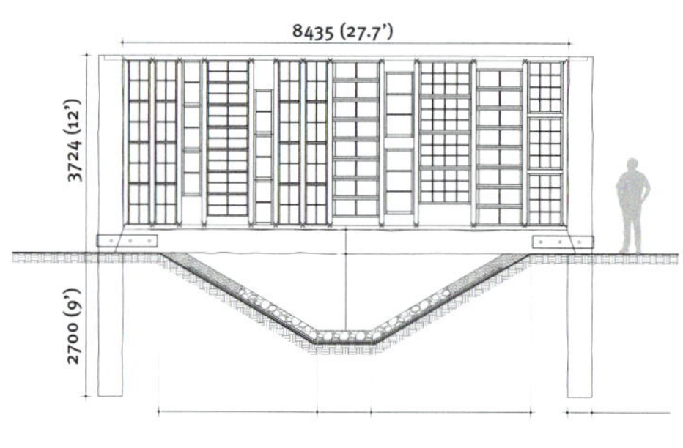

(2) Window frame type 2

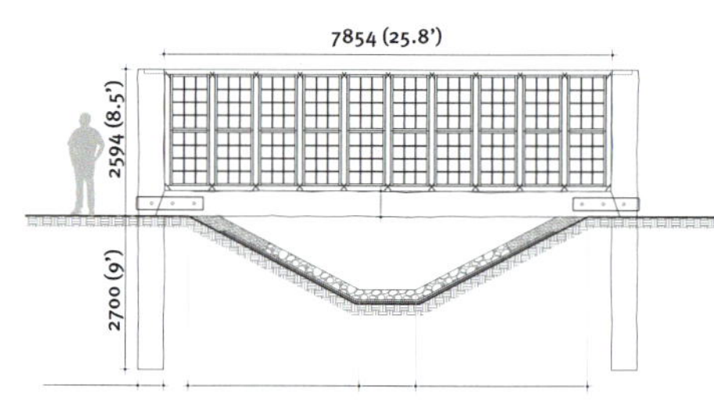

(3) Window frame type 3

The frames progress in height closer to the river.

"Most of the sites that we are working on today aren't conventionally beautiful, but this utilitarian ditch shows that we can find beauty in something quite ordinary."

Ken Smith

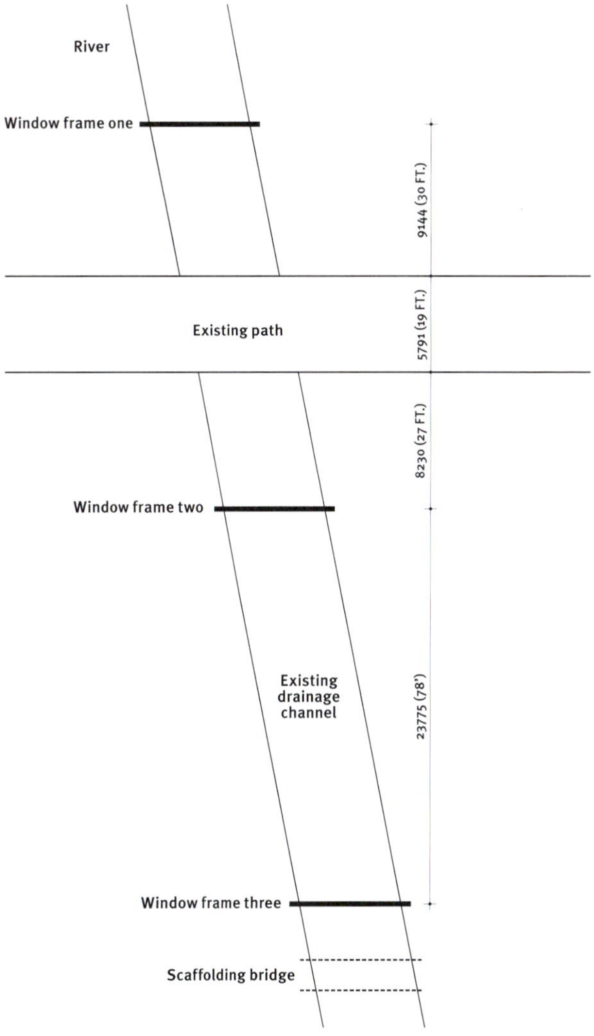

The frames bound secret garden spaces within.

MAKING CIRCLES IN THE WATER
Balmori Associates

2011–

Abstract

Making Circles in the Water experiments with visual perception of space to visually and experientially reconnect the Métis festival site with its surroundings.

Method

To turn our attention back toward the river—which has been separated from the gardens by the growth of shoreline vegetation—the installation uses two framing devices to manipulate how visitors apprehend the space and make the viewer more conscious of the act of seeing.

The first is a row of different-sized truncated plastic cones mounted along the shoreline. By looking through these cones, visitors have limited peripheral vision and a sharpened focus on the river horizon. These hand-held devices restrict the field of vision and allow visitors to experiment with different views, focal points, and even sounds as some visitors put the cones to their ears to magnify the sounds of the landscape.

The second device is a series of frames that offer an enlarged, full-body version of the cone experience. Designed to be walked through and explored, the apertures within the frames get smaller as they move toward the river, so as visitors walk through the frames, the field of view opens itself and the horizon gets wider, actively engaging us in considering the land and the river.

Result

As visitors actively engage with controlling and manipulating views of the St. Lawrence, they are given a clearer picture of the relationship between the river and the garden site and develop a higher awareness of the act of seeing.

Materials

Wooden frames, paint, and plastic cones

Visitors experiment with looking through the truncated plastic cones to create different relationships to the St. Lawrence River.

Limited peripheral vision through the cones and frames sharpens focus on the horizon.

Frames are painted in a gradient from dark to light to provide the highest contrast for the final river view.

"It just changes your perception once you know that that river is there. Once you re-integrate it with the site, the site feels much bigger and much more interesting."

Diana Balmori

For the 2015 edition of the festival, the frames are painted with an array of black and white lines leading to a central point on the horizon.

EDGE EFFECT
Snøhetta
2013–

Abstract
Edge Effect demarcates the threshold between the boreal forest and the neighbouring meadow ecosystems, focusing our attention on this narrow, but rich boundary zone.

Method
The edge zone is encircled by two asymmetrical steel arcs that rise from the ground as they approach the forest edge, offering a fluid interpretation of the transition from horizontal to vertical as we move from meadow to forest. This transition is also highlighted by the rope 'skirt' which descends from the high point of the structure back to ground level as it stretches out over the meadow.

The enclosed space creates an intimate room, transforming an abstract ecological concept into a destination where visitors can occupy and interact with the boundary zone. The rope mesh provides a hammock-like experience, allowing visitors different perspectives and relationships to the transitional zone.

A substantial underground foundation and a system of ground screws allow the steel structure to appear like it is floating above the landscape—an object poised to disappear as it is gradually integrated into the surrounding landscape. The maintenance protocol encourages this natural progression by allowing plants, debris, and unexpected growth to take over the structure.

Result
By creating a frame around this edge zone, the circular structure focuses our view on the textural transformation of the ground from forest floor to un-mown field, the spatial transition from horizontal to vertical, and the biodiversity of the boundary zone.

Materials
Steel structure, rope mesh, shade-tolerant forest-floor plants, meadow-mix seeds, slate gravel

Asymmetrical steel arcs highlight the threshold between forest and meadow landscapes.

The surrounding landscape begins to take over the structure.

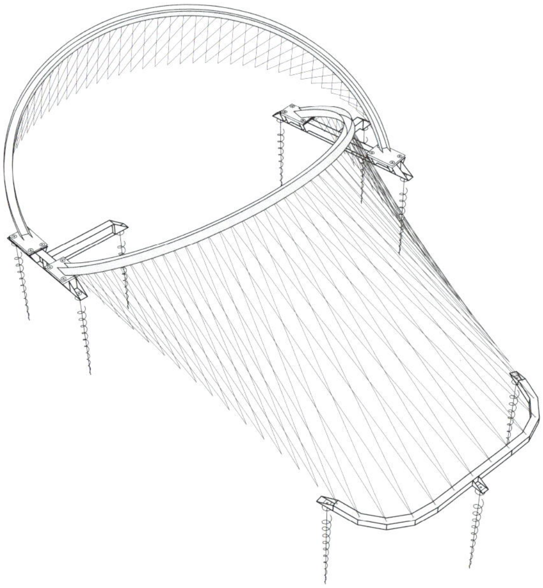

Ground screws and underground foundations (not pictured) allow the structure to float above the ground.

"Ecotones are a really exciting part of landscape. They're where a lot of biodiversity happens, they're where a lot of habitat happens. We really wanted to highlight that richness with this project."

Misako Murata

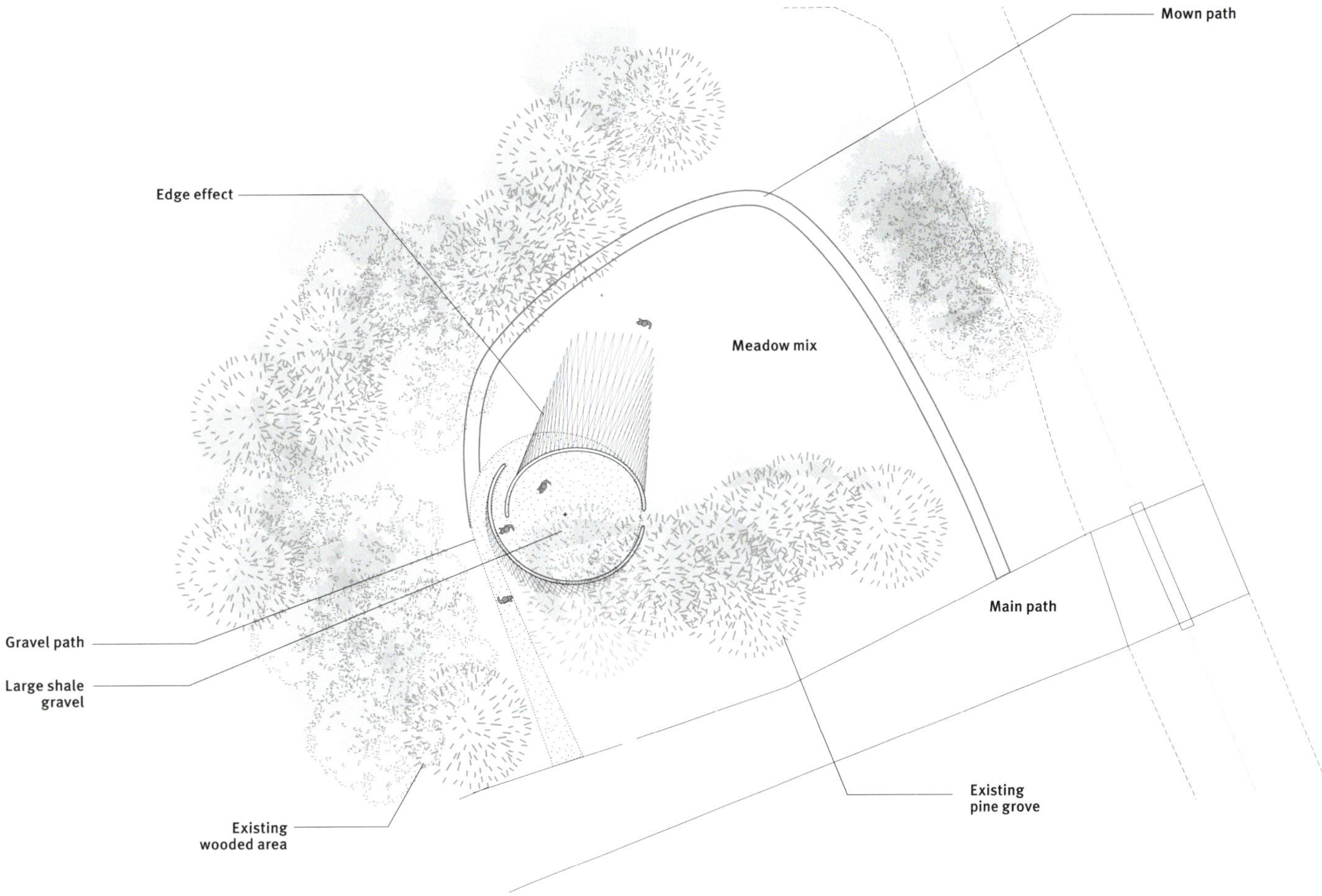

COURTESY OF NATURE
Johan Selbing and Anouk Vogel
2013–

Abstract
Courtesy of Nature encloses a section of the existing landscape and presents it in a gallery setting, asking visitors to take notice of the beauty of the environment around them.

Method
This garden does not design an object to be exhibited in the forest, but instead designs the exhibition space around existing elements. As the title suggests, the natural landscape itself is the exhibition and the designed elements are in service of viewing it more clearly.

As visitors walk down a woodland path, they approach a simple black volume that is almost camouflaged into its surroundings. As they pass through the threshold, they are surprised to find themselves in a stark white open-air gallery looking at a breathtaking exhibition of local trees and plants. The 'sculpture'—a double-trunked trembling aspen, a small spruce, ferns, and moss of the forest floor—grows out of the gallery floor and through an aperture in the ceiling, giving the appearance that the trees have been transported to a gallery. It is only when visitors realize that this is simply an isolated section of the same forest they just walked through, that they are struck by the real impact of this installation.

Result
Although the isolated trees are not remarkable among the other trees of the forest, by being placed in this gallery context, they become extraordinary and offer us a new way to perceive the existing environment.

Materials
Timber frame, white paint, black underlayment paper, gravel, existing trembling aspen, spruce, moss, ferns, rocks

Visitors enter the exhibition space to find a 'sculpture' growing through the gallery floor.

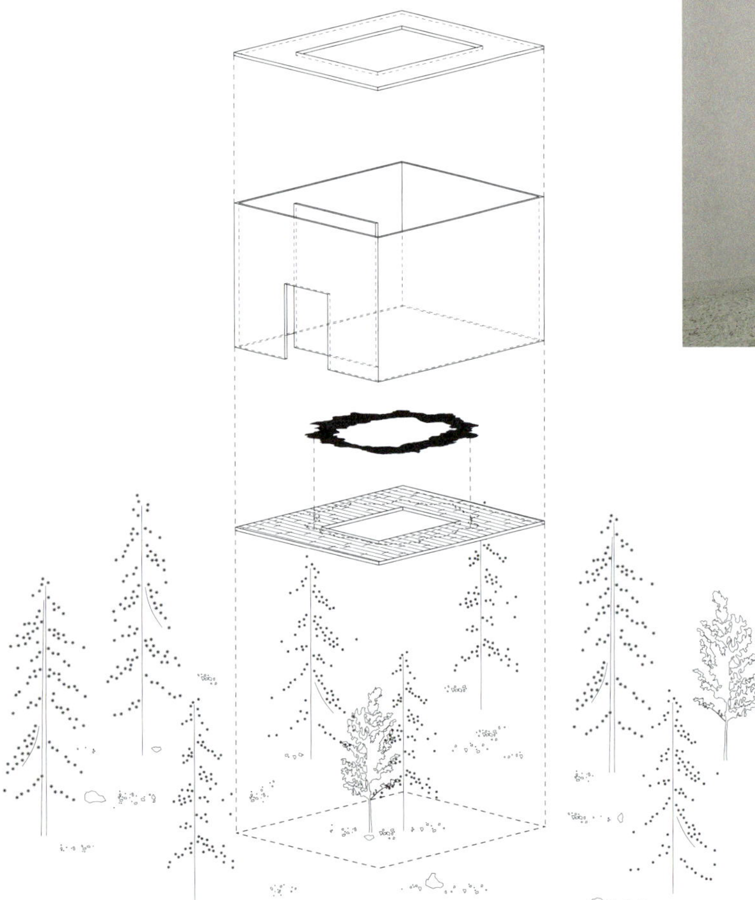

Exploded diagram showing layers of installation

"Often, natural elements become part of our daily lives so we tend not so see them anymore. Once you change the setting, people look at them again in complete amazement."

Anouk Vogel

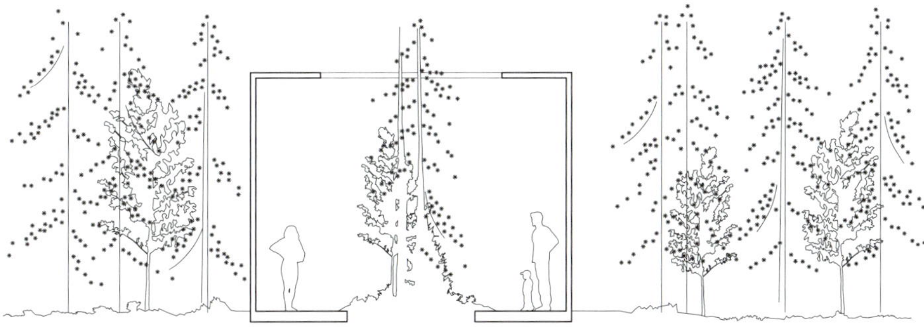

Visitors approach the garden on a woodland path.

The exhibition frames a double trunked trembling aspen, a small spruce, ferns, and moss of the forest floor.

RÉFLEXIONS COLORÉES

Hal Ingberg

2003–

Abstract

Réflexions colorées uses the constantly shifting conditions of the boreal forest to create an ever-changing perceptual experience. Instead of constructing a frame around an element of the landscape, this project becomes a frame on which to project and receive the conditions of the surrounding environment.

Method

The installation uses the chameleon-like properties of semi-reflective glass, which can appear transparent, translucent, or reflective, depending on the light conditions. Where a conventional mirror would stand out as an object in this environment, the coloured green glass adds to the ambiguity of the piece as it fades into the forest—designed to be barely visible unless you are consciously looking for it.

A 6 x 6-metre equilateral triangle of green semi-reflective glass interacts with the climate, atmosphere, materials, and light conditions of the forest to create a continually shifting perceptual experience. The experience of the piece will be completely different at 7am or at 5pm; it will be different again in spring when the reflections are much sharper and in the summer when the installation is softened by the appearance of leaves. A morning mist may turn the structure entirely translucent. At other times the forest may be projecting shadows onto an almost solid green wall.

Result

This 'machine for curiosity' provides visitors with as many different perceptual experiences of the forest as they are willing to go back to see. Each visit offers a new understanding of the climate, atmosphere, and light dynamics of the forest and is guaranteed to delight.

Materials

Green semi-reflective glass, forest, atmosphere, weather, light

Green semi-reflective glass interacts with the surrounding forest to create a continually shifting perceptual experience.

The installation appears different during each season and time of day, offering a new experience with every visit.

"It is really about experiencing the work in different ways throughout the day and through the seasons."

Hal Ingberg

ALTERED VIEWPOINTS

By observing something from a different vantage point, we can see even the most familiar things in a new way. This happened the first time we saw Robert Hooke's 1665 microscopic drawing of a flea, NASA's 1968 photograph of the entire earth from space, and Charles and Ray Eames' 1977 'Powers of 10' film. Each gave us new perspectives and deeper understandings of the scale of the universe and the earth's position in it by showing it to us from a different point of view.

By altering our visual relationships—vantage, zoom, scope, and focus—the gardens in this chapter offer us a new perspective in both senses of the word: as a view or a vista and as a mental outlook.

Some of these projects obscure our field of vision (*Camouflage View*), while others give us unexpected vantage points (*Tree Stands*, *Violence of the Garden*). Some change our physical relationships to familiar objects (*Dymaxion Sleep*) or allow us to occupy the garden in an unexpected way (*Around-About*).

In each case, a new vantage point offers us a new perspective, a deeper understanding, or a different perception of the environment around us.

CAMOUFLAGE VIEW
Aranda\Lasch
2005–2007

Abstract
Camouflage View distorts our reading of foreground and background to force a more considered exploration of the Métis site and its relationship to the St. Lawrence River.

Method
This garden uses the visually disruptive qualities of camouflage to hide the dramatic view of the St. Lawrence River in plain site and let it slowly reveal itself as visitors explore and discover on their own.

A serrated, mirrored wall built along the shoreline confuses the reading of foreground and background, making the view of the river appear in pieces as visitors move through the site. The wall is composed of reflective steel fins—the mirrored surface is angled to distort the foreground while slices in the fins reveal partial views of the background. The effect is momentary confusion while visitors navigate this constantly changing field of reflections and figure out exactly what it is they are looking at: a garden? The river? One's own reflection?

Once they finally reach the wall, the view is revealed, along with a concrete bench that offers a perch over the St. Lawrence River—a well-deserved reward.

Result
By obscuring what would otherwise be a straightforward view, this garden compels people to look more closely at what is around them, and as a result see the garden and its relationship to the river in a new way.

Materials
2.5-metre high laser-cut mirrored steel fins, hand-bent on site, concrete, castor oil plant (*ricinus communis*)

As visitors approach the wall, mirrored steel fins slowly reveal the St. Lawrence River beyond.

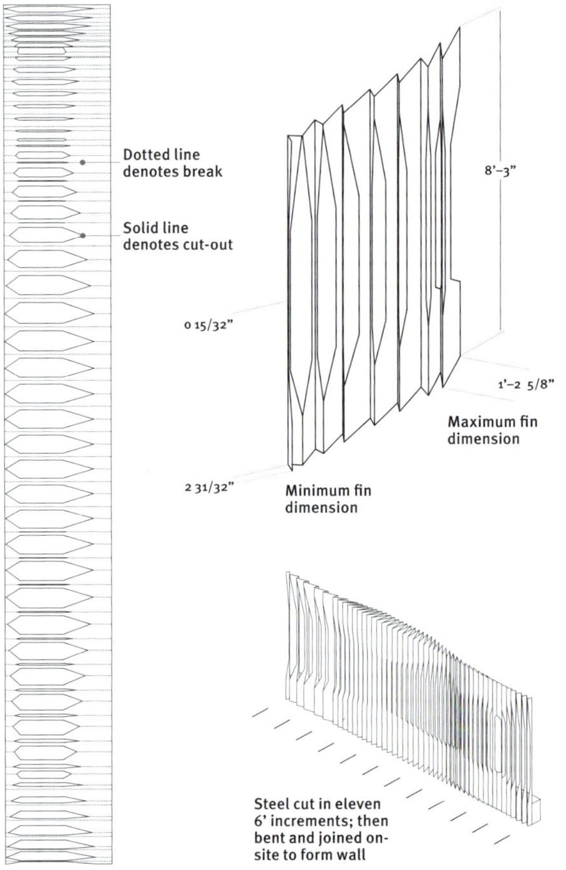

Laser cut steel fins are flat packed and are bent on site during installation.

"It was about trying to de-familiarize people to get them to pay attention to the site in a way that they otherwise might not have."

Chris Lasch

The wall is designed to 'hide the river in plain sight'.

TREE STANDS
relais Landschaftsarchitekten

2010 – 2011

Abstract

Tree Stands appropriates a traditional European hunting infrastructure to create a treetop perch where visitors can contemplate the sensations of the boreal forest.

Method

As woodland hunters wait silently in the trees, they develop a heightened awareness of their surroundings. Every smell, every sound, and every movement is amplified. This installation offers festival visitors the same sharpened focus on the local environment as they sit 3 metres (or 6 metres if they dare) up in the trees. From this elevated perspective, people will feel connected to the winds of the St. Lawrence River as the trees bend and sway beneath them, they will tune in to the shrill call of the white-throated sparrow, and will suddenly become very aware of the absence of civilization around them.

Without explicit directions, visitors will happen upon this curious collection of ladders in the forest and can choose whether to climb one of the two 3-metre-high stands or one of the four 6-metre ladders. From there, they can create their own experiences as they connect with the environment. Some visitors scramble up and down as many ladders as they can, others rest in one place, silently taking in this new perspective.

Result

By simply offering a different way to occupy the forest, *Tree Stands* provides visitors with an intensified awareness of the environment around them.

Materials

Trees cut and harvested on site

Visitors discover a collection of ladders in the forest and can choose to climb the 3-metre high stands or the 6-metre high ladders.

"From this unusual position, you are almost obliged to feel what is happening around you."

Gero Heck

Rope ladders are added for the 2011 edition of the festival.

VIOLENCE OF THE GARDEN (LAND USE OBSERVATORY)
Topotek 1
2010–2012

Abstract
Violence of the Garden uses the spatial language of war to demonstrate the aggression inherent in garden design.

Method
Creating a garden is a violent act. Soil is disturbed, existing trees, plants, and weeds are uprooted and a battle for ongoing control is declared. By using methods of transforming the landscape for the purposes of war, this garden highlights the dialectic between destruction and creation.

Visitors descend below grade into a wooden-slatted trench, where they are confronted at eye level with a grid of severed birch trunks and a tangle of barbed wire sprouting from a barren patch of soil. The birches remind us that in every garden there was something there before that must be removed to make room for the new. The barbed wire demonstrates the forceful exclusions we must make to maintain peace in the garden, and the barren soil can be seen either as destruction or as opportunity. In some cases it is dead and uninviting, whereas in others it sprouts with new life for pioneering plants.

From this sunken perspective, visitors can also look out to St. Lawrence River, whose often raging winds and frigid waters remind them of the potential violence of nature and the struggle in our attempts to control it.

Result
By physically and visually confronting visitors with the aggressive side of garden construction, *Violence of the Garden* forces us to consider the dialectic between the violence of creation and the idyllic peaceful gardens that we enjoy.

Materials
Birch trunks (diameter 10 to 15 centimetres, height 65 centimetres), barbed wire, wood panels

Within the trench, visitors are confronted at eyelevel with the markings of violence—a grid of severed birch trunks and a tangle of barbed wire sprouting from a barren patch of soil.

"There is connection between what your body experiences and your mind. When you go down steps, or you go up a ladder, there is a little insecurity, there's a risk. It's a combined experience between what you see and what you feel. You don't really think about it, but it reinforces your experience."

Martin Rein-Cano

A wireless connection is added for the 2011 edition of the festival.

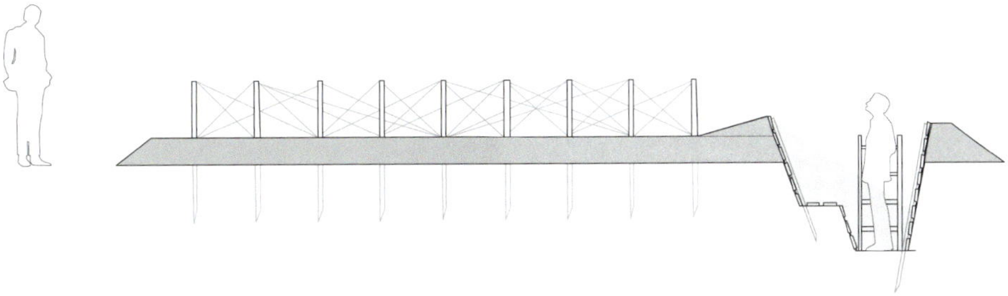

Elevation showing relationship of trench to ground level

DYMAXION SLEEP

Jane Hutton and Adrian Blackwell

2009–2013

Abstract

By changing how we occupy the garden, *Dymaxion Sleep* creates an unexpected and intense new relationship between garden visitors and plants.

Method

Beginning with a question about how people occupy (and possibly nap in) gardens and other public spaces, *Dymaxion Sleep* quickly became about intensifying the relationship between people and plants in a way that cannot happen when we simply walk between them on a typical garden visit.

The triangulated form—reminiscent of Buckminster Fuller's Dymaxion map—is an unfolded icosahedron, a three-dimensional solid with 20 equilateral triangle faces. In this installation, each of the faces is an almost immaterial netting that allows people to float above the aromatic garden below. Whether lying face to face with the plants or lying on your back 60 centimetres above them, you will feel the presence of the garden. The more you move around, brush against, and agitate the fragrant plants the more they release their aromas, creating a dynamic and interactive relationship between visitors and the garden below.

The 2011 iteration of the project, *Dymaxion Sleep* (*curled up*), re-folds the icosahedron offering new ways to occupy the structure, new relationships, and some much sought after shade.

Result

Just as Fuller's map created a different view of the world, *Dymaxion Sleep* invites different views of how to occupy the garden and the relationship between people and plants.

Materials

Tubular steel structure, nylon and polypropylene netting, timber footings, aromatic plants

An almost immaterial netting allows 'sleeping' visitors to float just above the aromatic garden below.

"The idea was that the plants would always have an influence on you, either visually or sensorially, but over time, people's bodies began to influence the growth of plants also. It made an intense relationship between the two."

Jane Hutton

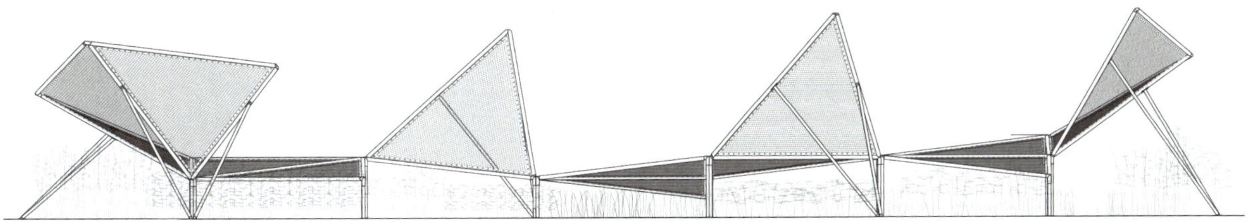

Site elevation facing south

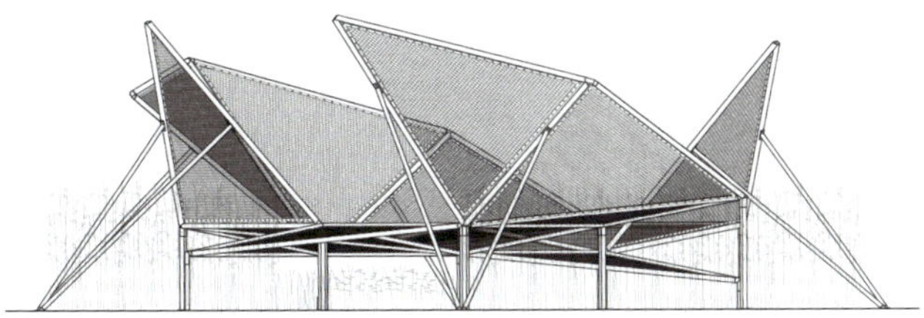

Site elevation facing east

Fennel (*foeniculum vulgare*)

Catmint (*nepeta faassenii*)

The aromatic plants release their scents as visitors brush up against them.

The icosahedron is folded up for the 2011 edition of the festival, offering new ways to occupy the structure.

AROUND-ABOUT
Talmon Biran architecture studio
2015–

Abstract
Around-About transforms visitors from passive viewers into active participants in the creation and evolution of the garden.

Method
Typically, a garden visitor observes a carefully choreographed landscape, designed for the pleasure and delight of the viewer. A design is implemented and begins its cycle of growth, blooming, and decay. *Around-About*, instead, relinquishes control of this process to the visitors by allowing them to actively change, alter, erase, and create new textures and patterns on the garden's surface.

Visitors arrive at a flat gravel field reminiscent of a Japanese Zen garden and are invited to activate one of the three huge steel carousels to create their own patterns as they drag the wheels across the gravel surface. The carousels—inspired by agricultural cultivating machines—range from 1.6 to 3 metres in diameter, and feature tines at different densities to allow varying patterns and textures.

A collection of hand-made wooden rakes, also of varying dimensions and with different densities of tines, encourage visitors to experiment with more free-form patterns and designs. Each new 'designer' must decide how to react to, cover up, or build upon the work of the previous visitor. When they are finished, they must disturb their own work as they walk across it to exit the garden, emphasizing the idea of order and disorder in garden design.

Result
By actively engaging visitors in the creation and transformation of the garden, *Around-About* offers a deeper connection and experience of the garden.

Materials
Gravel and wood chips, steel carousels (1.6, 2.3, and 3 metres diameter), wood and plywood rakes and benches, metal bushings

Visitors are invited to create their own patterns by spinning the large steel carousels.

Visitors are active participants in the transformation of the garden.

"We are fascinated with the relationship between the user and the appearance of the project. Like a performance in both senses of the word—how things operate, but also as a show. We are constantly searching for the relationship between these two meanings."

Roy Talmon and Noa Biran

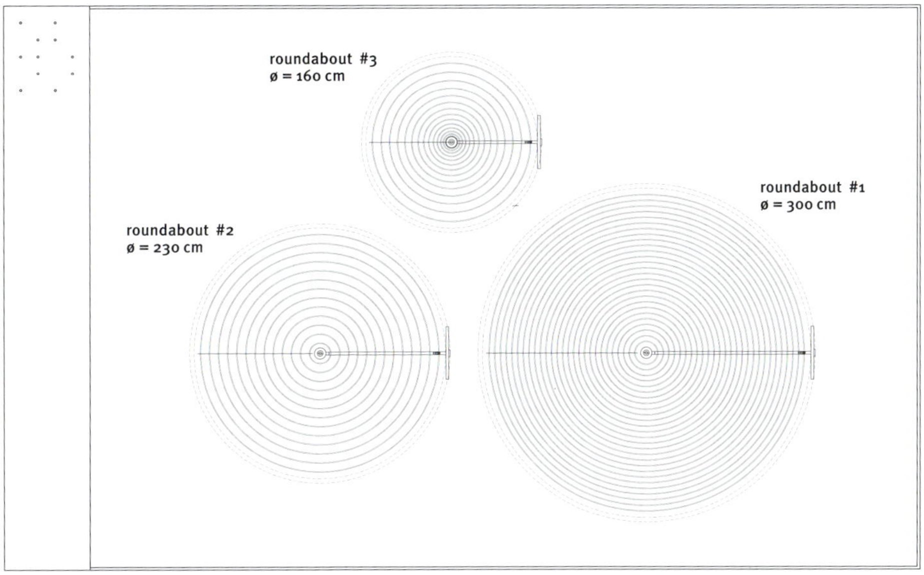

Site plan

Custom-designed rakes allow visitors to create varying patterns.

City and Nature Master Garden, Martha Schwartz Partners, Xi'an International Horticultural Exposition, 2011

SENSE OF PLACE VS. TABULA RASA: THE PARTICULAR AT MÉTIS

Tim Richardson

The proliferation of conceptual garden festivals through the 1990s and 2000s, which began to slow down only in about 2005, begs the question as to their particularity. What makes each festival different, or even unique? How do the installations sit within the landscape? After all, many of these festivals have been situated either in dynamic and stimulating natural environments, or else in the specific context of an historic estate. In the case of Métis, it is both.

Rigour is a key point in conceptualist art, in that the artist needs to be strongly disciplined and utterly clear when it comes to expression of ideas or concepts, whatever the medium being used. Conceptualist landscape design ought to be subject to the same level of interrogation. As a result, various questions might be posed with regard to this question of rigour, especially when it comes to the sense of place, or the landscape in which the work is cradled. For example, is there evidence of reverence, of a dialogue or a feeling of interwovenness? Or is there by contrast a sense of irreverence, a decisive rejection of the existing characteristics of the site in favour of the artist's 'unmediated' creativity? Or is it that many of the designers involved have taken neither approach, instead almost taking for granted the physical and conceptual context of the festival?

It must be admitted that in many cases and at different festivals this last path is the one which appears to have been followed most often, with designers working up their ideas in the comfort of the studio and treating the opportunity as an intellectual exercise, or as a way of 'playing' or 'experimenting with ideas'. Perhaps the process of accessing this creative 'freedom', of dreaming up ideas apparently without frontiers, has sometimes led designers and artists working in the landscape milieu to forget or to side-line what is often the greatest strength of their genre: the presiding 'sense of place', people's relationship with it, and how it might be manipulated, enhanced, or modified. The best conceptual designers—Martha Schwartz, Claude Cormier, Ken Smith, Kathryn Gustafson—tend to exhibit evidence of an engagement with the history of the site or locale in their work out in the 'real world'. When it comes to the conceptual garden festival, this sense of context is often eschewed in favour of the idea of the installation site as a tabula rasa, a blank page upon which anything might be written. A potentially rich seam of contextual inspiration and information is therefore written out of the equation at an early stage.

Indeed, the conceptualist landscape project seems to have largely 'played' itself out by around 2005, with a sense of the fairground at shows where the exhibits appeared to be beamed in from nowhere into a placeless and unparticularized site, and where the 'play' so relished by the designers involved could easily come across as superficial and/or self-indulgent. For some, the very concept of the 'show

Château de Chaumont and Festival International des Jardins

Carnivore Parc, Mathieu Allain and Stéphane Le Gourrierec, Festival International des Jardins 2015

En apesanteur, Luc Voisin, Jeanne Couaillier, and Mathieu Brison, Festival International des Jardins 2013

garden' began to feel rather 20th-century; hence the creation of the Chelsea Fringe model in London (2012–) in which sustainable ongoing projects are made or initiated in real places, while existing projects are re-energized and introduced to new audiences by means of imaginative events and happenings.

It now seems a little odd to be wondering whether every conceptual garden festival has displayed evidence of a conceptual engagement with the site itself, but the fact is, the majority have not pursued such an engagement. Perhaps the tone was set by the very first conceptual garden festival, founded in 1992 at the Château de Chaumont in the Loire Valley. There, the Belgian designers Jacques and Peter Wirtz (who went on to redesign the gardens in front of the Louvre) created a labyrinthine festival layout consisting of discrete hedged enclosures, visually separated from each other. There was no visual connection with the chateau itself or the surrounding landscape. The result is a festival where the installations are arranged one next to the other, like fairground attractions. Or like pictures and sculptures in a white-cube gallery, where the background is ... just background—recessional, vacuum-like, blank. The conceit was that a garden festival could be treated like an art exhibition, with each piece a stand-alone component.

It is true that the very nature of such festivals, and a key element of their artistic strength, has lain in the fact that they allow for experimentation, crossover, hybridity, liminality, flux, and experimentation. Artists and designers are typically invited to submit ideas and designs on a particular theme, and they relish the opportunity to explore intellectual ideas and concepts which may have been bubbling away for several years with no outlet. For professional landscape architects, it might come as a relief to be able to forget about existing site conditions for once and let one's imagination roam free. Most artists will do that anyway, trained as they are in the idea that the finished work must be defined by their own creative personality above all (as opposed to a bunch of trees and other plants). The result is that in many cases the landscape setting is understood as, at best, a frame in which an installation or art piece might profitably be set. The landscape provides the backdrop, not the context.

One might expect, after this rather critical retrospective introduction to conceptual garden festivals, that the Métis Festival is now to be presented as the trophy exception which proves the rule—the one festival where the installations have over the years consistently exhibited a strong if not occasionally profound engagement with the particular landscape milieu in which it sits. This is only partially true.

Elephants, Tim Bushe, Chelsea Fringe, 2013

Garden of Disorientation, naganjohnson and uncommon, Chelsea Fringe, 2012

Fernery in the Toilet, Anna Rose Hughes, Chelsea Fringe, 2013

Elsie Reford

The Long Walk, Reford Gardens

Eucalyptus Light and Shadow, Taylor Cullity Lethlean

The dramatic St. Lawrence River landscape

Souvent me souviens (Often Remembered), Deborah Nagan, Métis-sur-Sainte-Flavie, 2013

Over the years, many Métis designers have been selected by dint of their joyous and irreverent conceptual experimentation. In some cases a relationship with the site itself grew up almost incidentally, 'on site' as it were, while the installation was physically taking shape. But even this happy possibility was often circumvented at Métis because of its very remoteness and the limitations of designers' budgets: in many cases, designers and artists would come up with their ideas and plans for Métis having never visited the site, and even after they had been accepted into the festival, their installations were by necessity constructed largely in their absence, with the designers only descending on the festival site a week or so before it opened to the public. Given such constraints, an authentic engagement with the site was nearly impossible. Where such engagement has occurred, it has generally been hard won, which makes it all the more precious and powerful.

Indeed, despite the practical problems, it is fair to say that, encouraged by festival director Alexander Reford and his jury, a relatively high proportion of designers involved at Métis have sought to re-present in their work a meaningful engagement with the site, setting, and wider locale, as well as the history of the place. From the beginning, the festival was conceived as intimately bound up with the historic Reford Gardens, the landscape setting on the St. Lawrence River, and the wider milieu or locale of the Gaspé Peninsula. The festival garden itself is dramatically set, close to the huge St. Lawrence River which looks more like a sea to Europeans, with a rocky shoreline. A handful of installations over the years have attempted to grapple with the sheer scale and magnificence of this landscape. Those installations which are situated in the formal, gridded, open spaces near to the festival entrance often struggle to find a connection with the place, while those placed in the wooded spaces farther on tend to have a stronger relationship with the setting. The historic Reford Gardens—adjacent to the festival site but entirely separate—were largely the creation of Elsie Reford in the early decades of the 20th century and is another potential source of inspiration and context. The particular flavour of the wider area—the farm buildings, the character of the people, and the strong sense of relative isolation – has also proved inspirational to designers (notably the British designer Deborah Nagan, who has referenced local vernacular

Jardin territoire, Atelier Pierre Thibault

Blue Stick Garden, Claude Cormier + Associés

Un jardin en mer, Pierre Bourgault and Maxime Bourgault

Histoire sans fin ou Le bois dans tous ses états, Atelier eem, 2012

architecture in her Métis installations). Finally, the climate is also occasionally a factor for designers and artists at Métis, especially given the fact that the site is covered with snow for a large part of the year; Taylor Cullity Lethlean's meditation on eucalyptus leaves, realized in perforated Corten steel, has been perhaps the most effective snowbound piece, partly because snow and gum trees are not a natural pairing.

All of the above and more have a particularizing effect on the installations presented at Métis. The sense of place is very strong; artists and designers who come to Métis are often overwhelmed by the combination of elements and influences. This means it is impossible to understand the exhibits by means of photographs alone—something certainly achievable at certain other conceptual garden shows.

This habit of relating work to the setting was established in the early years of the festival, with installations such as *Jardin territoire* (2001) by Atelier Pierre Thibault, a poetic landscape paean to the biological and geological character of the Métis shoreline, realized as emblematic slithers of landscape, from salt marsh to sunken shore to cultivated wheat to virgin forest. The Métis installation which first made me properly appreciate the potential power of this natural landscape for designers was *Un jardin en mer* (2005) by Pierre Bourgault and Maxime Bourgault, an artist and an architect who erected two columns of salt on a tiny distant island in the St. Lawrence River. Viewable through binoculars installed on a lookout above the shoreline, this strangely compelling installation bore witness to a process of gradual disintegration, as the columns of salt were gradually washed away by the sea spray.

Another early Métis installation which elaborated on the theme of the natural setting, and which has become something of a 'classic' of the festival, is Hal Ingberg's *Réflexions colorées* (2003–). This piece stands as a mysterious meditation on the nature of the woodland at Métis, its semi-reflective glass walls seeming to make it simultaneously a part of the forest and not a part of it. A more minutely observed, Ruskinian approach to nature appreciation is on display in *Tiny Taxonomy* (2010–) by Rosetta Elkin, a series of shiny metal tubes, each containing a circular miniature 'garden' made from choice-drawn woodland plants culled from the forest floor. *Macro/Micro/Myco* (2015) by Peter North and his students at the University of Toronto consists of pyramidal structures designed to encourage and display the different stages of life of mushrooms and other naturally occurring fungi. And *Histoire sans fin ou Le bois dans tous ses états* (2012–) consists of five 'mutating and decomposing spaces' which are designed to speed up the natural processes of the woodland before our very eyes, as organized by the design team. These installations which encourage, investigate, and celebrate the natural life of the Métis landscape seem to be very much in tune with the cultural and artistic Zeitgeist (the Venice Art Biennale has recently been packed with trees, soil, and vegetation-based installations and artworks). One of the approaches to conceptual landscape design which has been essayed sporadically (notably at the conceptual show in Gothenburg, Sweden, in 2008) is the activation of spaces by means of performance. Perhaps these installations can be said to dramatize natural processes for our delectation and amazement.

I am aware that I have perhaps posited the idea of contextual or site-specific design as necessarily the best option for designers and artists at conceptual garden festivals. This is certainly not always the case, and I can think of several installations in different places which function extremely well as escapist fantasies that are either convincingly abstract or redolent of another time and place altogether. The work of Andy Cao and Xavier Perrot springs to mind in this regard—their poetic installations at Métis, the Cornerstone Festival, and elsewhere were truly transcendent experiences which needed no 'dialogue' with the place surrounding them. The big 'hit' of the first years of the Métis festival (and the first conceptual show garden to go on a world tour) was Claude Cormier's *Blue Stick Garden*. This was essentially an artistically nuanced optical illusion, also married in to the history of the garden by means of the use of different shades of blue, re-presenting the Reford Gardens' signature *Meconopsis* flowers. Among the other convincing installations at Métis which one could imagine seeing at almost any other location, were *Mobile Landscape Intervention Unit* (2004) by Mousse Architecture de paysage, an emergency gardening module (complete with bunk beds) created inside a shipping container which made a virtue of its very transportability; and *Pomme de parterre* (2007) by Iarocci, Ironside and Ross, which harnessed the electrical charge of 1,000 wired-up potatoes grown in an adjacent plot, thereby creating and broadcasting a strange sonic drone. At the intersection of art and garden, *Ombre* (2002) by LAND-I was one of the most striking and effective pieces, consisting of a series of 49 geometric incisions in the forest floor, carpeted with grass and flowers within. These are among my personal 'greatest hits' at Métis, and they could just as effectively have been presented at Cornerstone, Westonbirt, or one of the other festivals.

The 'elephant in the room' at Métis is the political context. It seems strange that in a place as politically contested as Québec, where the Reford Gardens themselves stand as an important part of that political history, this aspect of the culture has not been addressed in the installations at the festival. An engagement with the recent history of Québec and its place within or without Canada, coupled with relations between the Anglophone and the Francophone communities, has proved somewhat too hot to handle, it would appear. To the outsider, the Métis Festival stands as a shining example of fruitful collaboration between people from all strands of Canadian society, so one can perhaps understand an inbuilt reluctance to pick away at a wound which is still in the process of healing. But on the other hand, shouldn't art also cause trouble on occasion?

An important characteristic of Métis, and one of its chief particularities, is the fact that it was very much the vision of one man, Alexander Reford, whose great-grandmother was Elsie Reford, creator of the historic gardens. Her obsessions were gardening and salmon-fishing, while Alexander's is palpably the conceptual garden festival. The place is so remote and the conditions so harsh that the entire enterprise could almost be accounted a folly, were it not for its national

Ombre, LAND-I

Mobile Landscape Intervention Unit, Mousse Architecture de paysage

Le Jardin des Hespérides, CAO PERROT

and international success, the respect its director is now accorded. Perhaps it would be more accurate to describe the Métis Festival as truly 'pioneering' in this territory. The role and power of the curator has recently become an important topic in the mainstream art world, and Reford's role should certainly be considered in this light—and all the more so given the fact that he occupies a liminal position both physically (in terms of the remoteness of Métis) and artistically, in that many in the art world would be reluctant to acknowledge Métis as an art show at all. But if one accounts for the determined internationalism of the festival and its genuinely avant-garde stance—which allows plenty of room for the acceptance of failure—then Reford perhaps ought to be considered a curator-artist in his own right. He is the director of an annual 'performance' that involves designers, technicians, garden staff, and visitors, including the local community. The Métis Festival is both a catalyst for creativity and a developing work of art in its own right.

Cyclops, Craig Chapple, Métis International Garden Festival, 2016

UNEXPECTED MATERIALS AND FORMATS

Over time, we come to expect certain things from the materials and objects we know well: grass grows on the ground, walls are vertical, and potatoes don't make sounds.

But, as is frequently demonstrated in the art world, upending our expectations of these everyday things, can completely change our perception of their functions, their value, and their meanings. Sometimes just by seeing familiar materials presented in unexpected ways, such as Marcel Duchamp's ready-mades or Damian Hirst's diamond-encrusted skull or seeing a familiar object reformatted like Rachel Whiteread's plaster-cast houses, our understanding of them is changed forever.

The gardens in this chapter offer new insights and associations by challenging our expectations of the way certain materials and objects perform. The results are provocative, surprising, and in many cases, delightful.

These projects use familiar materials in unfamiliar ways (*Pomme de parterre*, *Dead Garden II*), construct new formats using familiar elements (*Surface Deep*, *Round Up*), or reimagine familiar formats using new materials (*Sacré potager*).

POMME DE PARTERRE

Angela Iarocci, Claire Ironside, and David Ross

2007–2010

Abstract

Pomme de parterre puts a common garden plant (the potato) to an uncommon use (a sonic signal) to give a voice to this Canadian pantry staple.

Method

Pomme de parterre highlights the latent potential of the potato by showcasing its diversity and its power as a source of electricity. Visitors enter through a formal parterre garden where each section exhibits one variety of local heritage potato. As they explore this diverse collection of heritage plants, they begin to hear a curious buzzing sound coming from a sunken shed at the rear of the garden. As visitors descend into this underground chamber, it takes them a moment to identify the source of the strange sound: a giant battery constructed from 1,000 locally farmed potatoes.

The electricity produced by the relay-wired potatoes is converted to a sonic signal and broadcast into the room as variable buzzing tones. The sounds range from the lowest buzz of a dial-up modem up to the high-pitched chirp of a smoke detector whose batteries are dying. This rich, three-dimensional chorus is produced by individually tuning each section of the battery to issue its own tone, beep, buzz, or chirp. Over the course of the installation, the character of the drone will change as the potatoes are drained of their energy.

The sunken shed—reminiscent of local, vernacular agricultural buildings—was constructed on a foundation of potato shipping crates and functioned as a root cellar, keeping the potatoes cool through the summer months.

Result

By bringing such a common element to such an unexpected use, this garden continually surprised and delighted visitors, who were struck that something so ubiquitous could become so extraordinary.

Materials

200 kg locally sourced potatoes (approx. 1,000), potato shipping crates, piezo speakers, and specialized circuit boards

A sonic signal is powered by a battery made of approx. 1,000 potatoes, the number the average Canadian family consumes annually.

"We weren't interested in the sounds that typically go with gardens—wind chimes, babbling brooks, etc. We were interested in making a sound with something that doesn't make a sound."

Claire Ironside

<ins>Potato varieties</ins>
Norland
Matsuyama
Mrs. Moehrle's Yellow-Fleshed
Siberian, Papa Negra
Corne du Mouton
Elmer's Blue
Rode Eersteling
La Crotte d'Ours
Ailes Roses
Bauer Grün Rote Auge
Kifelĉer (Slovenian Crescent)
Bintje

<ins>Border plantings</ins>
Dwarf French marigold
Nasturtiums—trailing (Fordhook Favourites mix)

Visitors enter through a formal parterre garden featuring twelve varieties of local heritage potatoes.

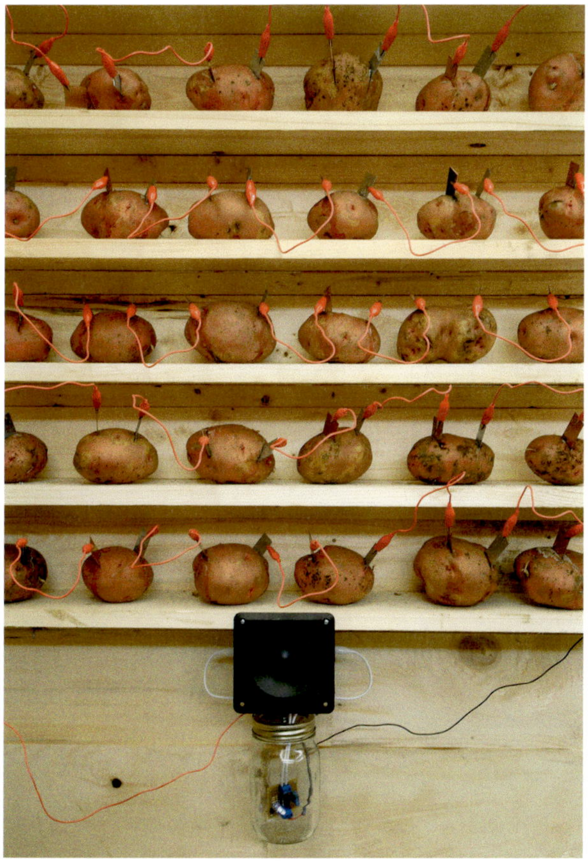

The battery is divided into 12 banks, each broadcasting a different tone via a specialized low amperage piezoelectric speaker.

DEAD GARDEN II
Carlos M. Teixeira
2013–

Abstract
Dead Garden II takes what we usually think of as garden waste (dead trees) and presents them as primary planting materials, asking us to reconsider the life cycle of the materials we use to design gardens.

Method
As the title suggests, *Dead Garden II* is constructed from dead material—fallen cedar logs found on the Métis Festival site. The bare logs are suspended horizontally from a timber frame to create a sequence of four corridors for visitors to move through, touch, and investigate the textures of the dead trees. The logs are suspended from ultra-thin wires, creating the feeling of a dynamic, flowing space.

The field of logs is framed and divided by white netting which defines the corridors and gives a sense of depth to the space. The netting itself comes to life by displaying haunting silhouettes and unexpected shadows. Ultimately, the bare surfaces of the logs are intended to grow moss, demonstrating how the death of one element creates life in another.

Result
By presenting us with a new use for a familiar material, *Dead Garden II* demonstrates how we can bring life to the garden with what we might otherwise consider a lifeless material.

Materials
Fallen cedar logs found on site, steel cords, timber frame, mosquito netting

Cedar logs are suspended horizontally from a timber frame, bringing life to an otherwise 'dead' material.

The field of logs is framed with white mosquito netting to add depth and texture to the space.

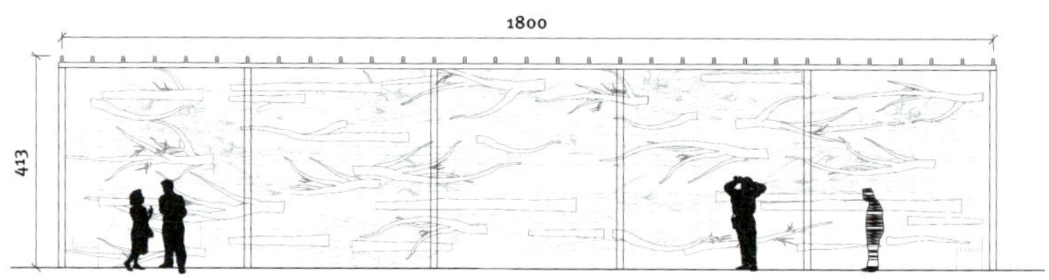

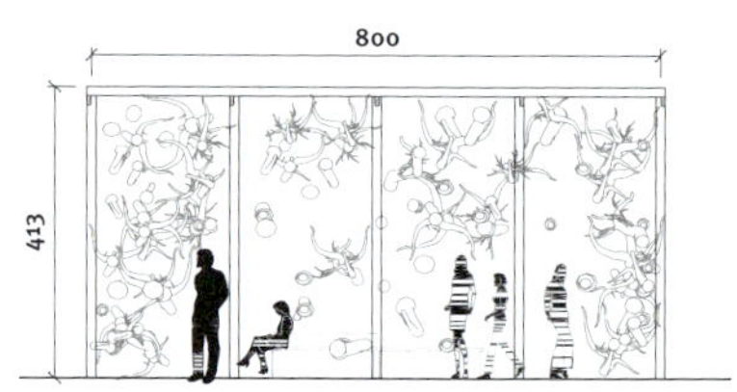

Elevations

"There was intention to simulate a flow with the way the logs are hung and the corridors promote movement through the space as they do in architecture."

Carlos M. Teixeira

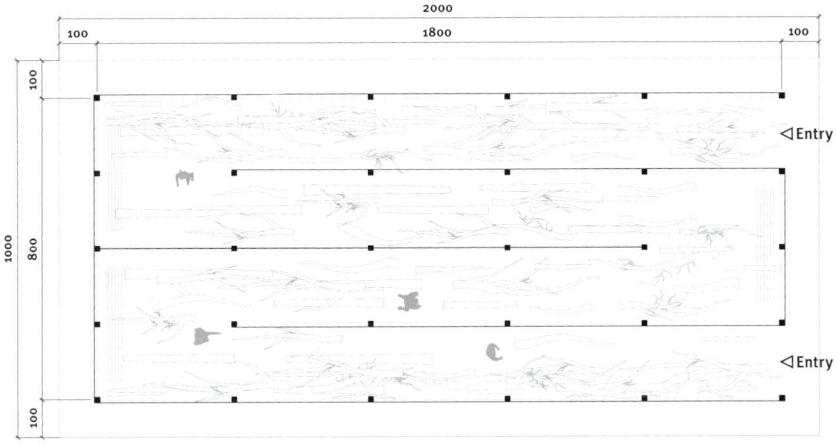

Layout plan

Four corridors choreograph movement through the garden.

SURFACE DEEP

asensio_mah with the Harvard University Graduate School of Design

2011–2014

Abstract

Surface Deep reformats the traditional garden wall, inviting new ways to engage with and occupy this familiar structure.

Method

Instead of using a wall to frame the garden, *Surface Deep* re-defines the wall as the garden itself.

Unlike the typical garden wall, the angle of this wall fluctuates, creating different relationships with the ground along its length. Sometimes it is vertical like a traditional wall, and sometimes it is more horizontal as it tilts overhead or leans away from you. These different conditions create various micro-climates (enclosure, sun exposure, and surfaces for occupation) offering a variety of ways for people and mosses to colonize the wall.

Different species of moss are distributed along the fluctuating surface, ranging from sun-tolerant mosses on the upturned faces to those that prefer the darker and more humid conditions as the wall tilts toward the ground. Because the plant material is embedded into the surface (unlike the traditional garden wall which simply frames the plants), people are enticed to come over and touch it, explore it, and even contort their bodies to take a closer look.

The wall is constructed with angled plywood frames that are faced with a CNC-milled surface containing individual trays to grow the moss. The cellular pattern on the face of the wall breaks the large surface into smaller pockets which retain moisture levels and provide shading for the moss.

Result

This reformulation of the traditional garden wall invites a more intense level of engagement and changes our understanding of the role of the wall in the garden.

Materials

Marine-grade plywood, CNC-milled composite panel, concrete pad, steel anchors, peat-moss substrate, loose gravel chips, steel plates

The fluctuating angle of the garden wall creates different relationships with the ground along its length.

The cellular structure helps to maintain moisture levels and provides shade for the plant material.

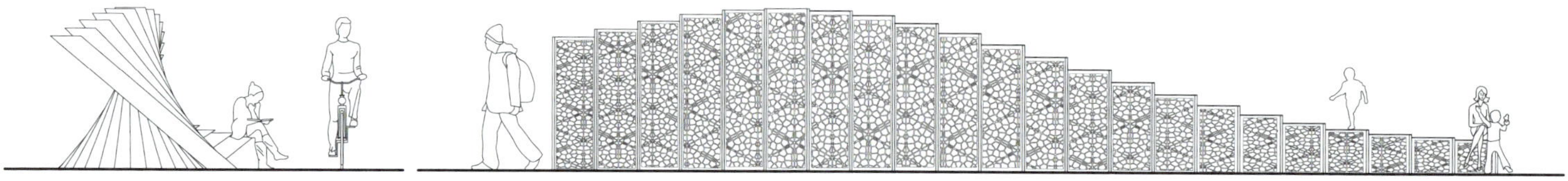

Elevations

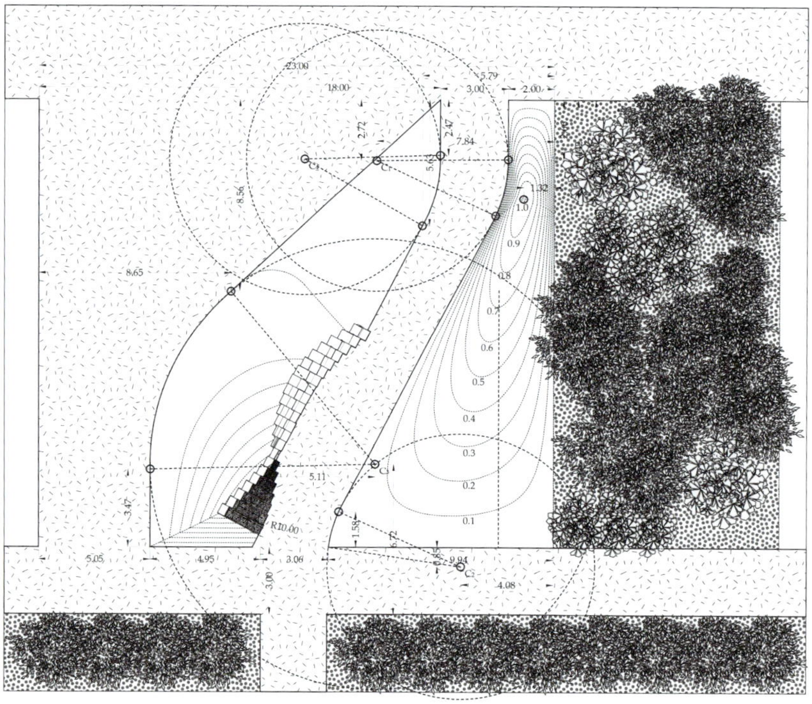

Site plan

"We are interested in a different relationship between form and function. If we take an element associated with gardens and make a slight change to the way that it's organized, we might invite different ways of engaging with it."

David Mah

Two undulating landforms planted with native flowers and grasses flank the wall structure and provide an inviting and casual entryway to the festival site.

ROUND UP

Legge Lewis Legge

2008–2010

Abstract

Round Up pushes an everyday landscape material to its extreme to create a surprising experience for visitors.

Method

This project begins where most building projects end—with a delivery of sod arriving strapped to a truck. In an act of 'extreme landscaping', *Round Up* reconfigures the traditional lawn to do the opposite of what we expect. Instead of lying flat on the ground, these almost 2-metre-high 'lawns' stand vertically, held together only by the trucking straps that secured their transport to the site. They simultaneously defy our expectations of turf and our expectations of gravity.

Where traditional lawns remain uniform through maintenance, these turf hills are designed to grow and change over time. When they are first constructed, the machined-looking hills are nearly identical, but over time they take on their own identities as they slump, shift, and grow into individual characters.

Eventually, the grass overgrows the strapping, leaving an odd-looking collection of landscapes that invite a closer look to try to figure out just how they got here. In the final year of the installation, the forms were seeded with wildflowers and a jaggedly meandering beam that gave visitors a new way to interact with the installation.

Result

The tension in this garden between the ubiquitous and the unexpected, the constructed and the natural, the possible and the impossible leaves visitors with a feeling of curiousity, surprise, and delight.

Materials

Sod, polyester truck strapping, steel cam buckles, soil

As they grow and shift, these vertical lawns simultaneously defy our expectations of turf and our expectations of gravity.

For the 2010 edition of the festival, two serpent-shaped beams invite visitors to explore the vertical wildflower meadow.

The turf hills are constructed from soil and sod held together by trucking straps.

"The way sod is cut, its uniformity, the hybridization of the plant material, the way it comes on palettes—it really becomes like an industrial building material."

Murray Legge

SACRÉ POTAGER
Atelier Barda
2013–

Abstract
Sacré potager (Sacred Garden) repurposes the traditional church shrine to bring attention to the disappearance of local heritage vegetables.

Method
As modern agricultural processes become more efficient and globalized, heirloom vegetable varieties have been weeded out in favour of 'superior' high-yield, disease-resistant, and easy-to-ship hybrids. By presenting 18 species of these 'forgotten' vegetables as objects of worship, *Sacré potager* brings our attention back to these heritage varieties and offers a wink to the current grocery culture that has elevated these rare breeds from the profane to the sacred.

The garden features 18 white mini-chapels or altars, each devoted to one heritage species. The vegetable itself is planted at the base of the altar while its hand-drawn image is emblazoned on a collection of votive candles reminiscent of those used in church shrines.

The candles also reveal the origin story and history of each vegetable, such as the *Trail of Tears* bean, which survived the deadly 1,750-kilometre march as the Cherokees were forcefully relocated to Oklahoma. Or the *Tante Alice* cucumber, which would have died with its breeder in 2005, if not for the five tiny seeds that were saved by her family. These narratives point to the sacred role of food in our society and show us that the stories of these vegetables are the stories of human history.

Result
By seeing this plant material presented in this sacred format, we are forced to consider the importance of their role in our history and culture, and confront our own relationship to our food sources.

Materials
Painted plywood, sheet metal and goldleaf, 1,200 votive candles, heritage vegetables

A collection of mini-chapels are devoted to the preservation of endangered heritage vegetables.

Trail of tears bean (*phaseolus vulgaris*)
Boston marrow squash (*cucurbita maxima*)
Jerusalem artichoke (*helianthus tuberosus*)
Chinese artichoke (*stachys affinis*)
Currant tomato (*solanum pimpinellifolium*)
Garden pea (*pisum sativum*)
Canada crookneck (*cucurbita moshata*)
Cucumber Tante Alice (*cucumis sativus*)
Indian Strain tomatillo (*physalis ixocarpa*)
New Zealand spinach (*tetragonia tetragonioides*)
Perennial wall rocket (*diplotaxis tenuifolia*)
Skirret (*sium sisarum*)
Tomato Dr Carolyn (*solanum lycopersicum*)
Marmande tomato (*solanum lycopersicum*)
Common bean (*phaseolus vulgaris*)
Kale (*brassica oleracea var. viridis*)
Common ice plant (*mesembryanthemum crystallinum*)

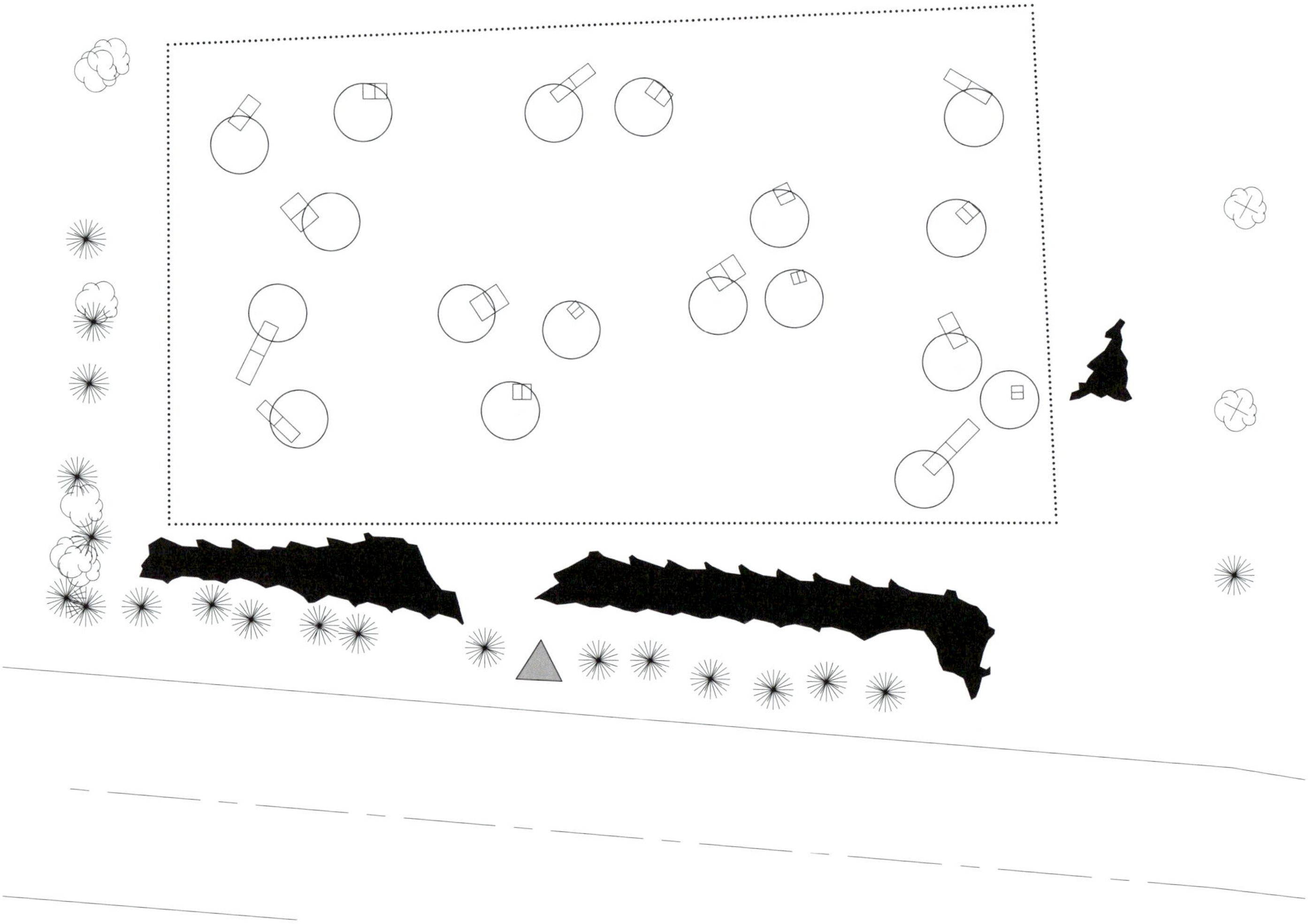

Planting plan

"Humans have always built monuments to worship the sacred, but over time the notion of what is sacred has evolved."

Cécile Combelle

Visitors are invited to make a donation to light a prayer candle to save the vegetables.

Each vegetable species is represented on hand-painted votive candles and in a small garden below.

Spiral Jetty, Robert Smithson

THE EXPERIMENTAL GARDEN AS AN EXERCISE OF PRACTICE

Marc Hallé

Gardens have always been places of experimentation. Gardeners continually test the limits of their plots to comprehend and work with the continually changing characteristics that are unique to each. Understanding these limits, however, is more than just figuring out site-specific agronomic parameters, such as sun and shade, or soil quality and moisture. Culture too is a fundamental parameter among these. And as an agent of culture, the garden becomes a canvas for cultivating ideas. Experimental gardens such as those at the International Garden Festival at Métis have been critical in giving designers a free space to focus solely on the exploration and expression of the idea.

Like a work of art, the experimental garden is an experience of ideas that provokes new insights about the world around us. At the same time, the experimental garden is more than merely a work of art. It is also an exercise of practice, giving designers the opportunity to define and refine a conceptual working method for doing landscape architecture. Free from program and function, the experimental gardens at Métis invite designers to distill and advance the attitude of practice that is manifest in their larger urban work. Many of the projects created by Métis alumnae beyond the festival are consistently distinguished by their use of concept and narrative to navigate through a landscape of grey zones where many truths are possible, and to create a coherent framework for making decisions. This essay explores how the ideas distilled by designers in their experimental gardens at Métis reflect this framework and reveal the conceptual essence found at the heart of their larger urban work beyond the festival and out in the world.

FROM FUNCTION TO FICTION IN LANDSCAPE ARCHITECTURE

In the 1970s, the dictum 'form follows function' prevailed in many schools of landscape architecture. Design was understood as a rational practice of linear logic, and any priority for place making was overwhelmed by a momentum toward standardization and homogeneity. In contrast, during this period, place and the *idea* in the landscape were reinforced by the rise of land artists such as Robert Smithson, Walter de Maria, and James Turrell. These figures are among the first to reassert courageously landscape as an artistic force of culture and expression. Smithson's *Spiral Jetty*, a work of relocated earth and rock bulldozed into the shape of a spiral protruding off the shore of Great Salt Lake, is probably the most enduring and well-known work of the 1970s land artists, and has become particularly emblematic of this movement.

Bagel Garden, Martha Schwartz

In landscape architecture, the resuscitation of concept as art and culture made a quiet debut in 1980 when a young landscape architect named Martha Schwartz laid out an array of bagels on purple gravel in the front garden plot of her Boston home. Dismissed by many at the time as folly, the *Bagel Garden* unexpectedly became the start of a conceptualist movement where art, intuition, and narrative reinforced landscape architecture as an autonomous agent of culture. The ramifications of Schwartz's *Bagel Garden* breakthrough have been far-reaching, enabling contemporary practitioners to wield concept and narrative as practical approaches in dealing with complex real-world problems.

This transition in practice from "form follows *function*" to "form follows *fiction*" is the undercurrent which has made contemporary garden festivals like Métis so relevant. This exercise in ideas shapes a practice of narrative where a logical framework is set up to trace links between design moves and their intended consequences. More than mere conceptual storytelling, this narrative is helpful for weaving a plausible fiction from the myriad characters, settings, dispositions, and phenomena that make up the landscape continuum. This narrative provides a vehicle for the imagination to leap beyond the inertia of a given reality, synthesizing elements of the 'story' into a tangible drama through forms, objects, and the relationships engendered by their spatial arrangement. Liberated from functional pressures, Métis becomes a laboratory for composing these fictions, either for emerging designers to define their voices, or for seasoned practitioners to advance and affirm the priority of the idea at the core of their practice.

CULTIVATING AN ATTITUDE OF PRACTICE

One example of the way the Métis Festival enables emerging firms to define their rhythms of practice can be found in the architecture studio of Aranda\Lasch. This firm considers their 2005 Métis garden *Camouflage View* (pages 78–81) as *the* formative project in figuring out their approach to design. At Métis, they were able to develop an agility and precision in computer-aided design to create a sophisticated piece of poetic complexity. This experience has carried over into their other work, such as *20 Bridges for Central Park*, where a new typology of fractal organic structures would dissolve not only barriers to park circulation, but also the separation between nature and construct as well as function and expression. Without the liabilities, technical specifications, and functional constraints demanded by bigger and more permanent projects, Métis has been able to offer exposure for younger talent, such as Aranda\Lasch, to incubate their emerging design personality and gain confidence in their position towards practice.

***20 Bridges for Central Park*, Aranda\Lasch**

Another example of Métis as a laboratory for emerging designers is the *Blue Stick Garden*, by Claude Cormier, installed during the inaugural edition of the festival in 2000. In Cormier's larger urban work that has ensued over the growth of his practice, the *Blue Stick Garden* continues to give insight into the fundamental principles that have endured at the core of his practice. When he was a student at Harvard University, Claude Cormier worked in the office of Martha Schwartz where he witnessed how art and experience could be elevated as priorities in creatively synthesizing site, context, history, planting, and colour into an emerging landscape method.

The conceptual genesis for the *Blue Stick Garden* invokes the history of the Reford Gardens itself. Elsie Reford had been inspired by Edwardian gardens when she created her own gardens on the banks of the St. Lawrence River. An enduring feature of her work is the double herbaceous border, the Long Walk, a garden that is richly planted on both sides of a central walkway with low groundcovers in front transitioning to taller plating in back. The result is a compact yet spacious allée, dynamically activated by the movement of the visitor and the blooming succession of flowers over the season. Crossbreeding this 19th-century precedent with 21st-century phenomena like digitalization, pixellated reduction, and mass replication, the *Blue Stick Garden* produced an experience rooted in both the specificity of the historic gardens in Métis as well as a futuristic universality that is authentically meaningful to a contemporary audience. The colour, blue, is also a site-specific reference, taken from the Himalayan blue poppy (*Meconopsis betonicifolia*) that Elsie Reford adapted to the local micro-climate, and which has become the symbol of the Reford Gardens. The spontaneous and inspired mashup of these fundamental starting points is synthesized by injecting a colour counterpoint taken from the blue poppy itself—the orange of the flower's central pistil—to stimulate contrast and accent against the signature blue of the garden.

The combination of these two chromatic opposites is strategically arranged to optimize the visual power of their juxtaposition. Orange is deployed primarily on the fourth face of each stick opposite the entrance to the garden, rendering the continuous field of blue upon entry into a sudden transformation to orange at the garden's cul-de-sac. Visitors performing the 180 degree turn at the end of the garden can be heard exclaiming "*Mon Dieu!*" at the unexpected shock of the colour change. The interplay between the deliberate *camaïeu* of orange and blue on the return through the garden simulates the dynamic blooming sequence of a whole season through a kind of evocatively choreographed striptease.

This small conceptual garden embodies an inspired hybrid that underlies the working method in much of Claude Cormier's work: a creative interpretation of history, impressionistic yet faithful engagement with context and site, emphasis on universal phenomena to arouse visceral appeal, an emphasis on pleasure and desire, a non-decorative use of colour, and a starting point of humour toward a serious conclusion of depth. A similar hybridization is observed at *Sugar Beach*, which opened on the Toronto Waterfront in 2010, where the importance given to the organizing idea was fundamental in galvanizing the project's conceptual integrity against the vicissitudes of financial, technical, political, and construction constraints.

Blue Stick Garden, Claude Cormier + Associés

Sugar Beach, Toronto, Claude Cormier + Associés

The first principles behind the narrative for *Sugar Beach* are based on the site's adjacency to a fully operational sugar factory on the opposite quay. Like Elsie Reford's mixed border garden and the Himalayan blue poppy at Métis, the sugar factory acts as a historical hinge between the site's gritty past and its post-industrial future. The "*Mon Dieu!*" moment is built into the spatial arrangement of key features such as the beach and tree-lined promenade, where a 180 degree turn of the gaze here creates a sudden and unexpected transition between the vertiginous verticality of the city skyline to the north and the exaggerated horizontality of the Lake Ontario horizon to the south. Like the *Blue Stick Garden's* conceptual narrative that reaches forward through time by digital-era representation and replication, the scheme at *Sugar Beach* reaches across dimensions where the spectacle of gantry cranes offloading raw cane sugar from tankers in the slip is reinforced by the feel of brown sugar-like sand under foot and the smell of raw sweetness in the air.

Superkilen, Copenhagen, Topotek 1, Bjarke Ingels Group, and Superflex

Superkilen, Copenhagen, Topotek 1, Bjarke Ingels Group, and Superflex

TENDING A WORKING PHILOSOPHY

In addition to enabling emerging designers to define a working method, Métis also provides a space for established practices to evolve and reconsider their own conceptual positions. This is evident in the garden of another Métis alumnus with a large repertoire of remarkable public work, the Berlin landscape architecture firm Topotek 1. The firm's installation at Métis in 2010, *Violence of the Garden* (pages 86–89), conveys a social and political position that has become part of Topotek 1's attitude of practice. Many of Topotek 1's earlier projects are distinguished by their saturation of colour, pattern, and creatively pragmatic flexibility of use. However, *Violence of the Garden*—a statement about the garden as a site of conflict, negotiation, and strategy—at first appears as a conceptual departure from their early work. It portrays landscape as a non-neutral agent underlying a contested territory of competing interests, with garden tools as weapons and barbed wire manifesting entitlement and power for asserting boundaries and appropriating geography.

The contemporary work of Topotek 1 has become fearless in taking sides. It optimistically provokes conflict in a way that transcends contention, using difference to reveal a counterintuitive universality. An empathetic audacity distinguishes their work, challenging habits of entitlement to reclaim an understanding of landscape as shared commons unencumbered by habits of privilege.

The constructive cultivation of conflict condensed in *Violence of the Garden* is manifest at the conceptual heart of *Superkilen*, a project opened in 2012 through a collaboration with Topotek 1, Bjarke Ingels Group, and the arts organization Superflex. The project is located in an ethnically diverse quarter of Copenhagen where 99 percent of the residents are from outside Denmark, and low levels of income and education prevail. The conceptual narrative employed here aims to relieve stigmatization and cultivate new understandings by creating a space for 'coming out', where the neighbourhood's diversity is brought out of the shadows, and the identity of the neighbourhood's inhabitants becomes the public space through a loud maximization of difference. The 108 elements that fill the park were curated with the residents of the neighbourhood, who put forward an authentic, symbolic, and personally meaningful palette of cultural objects that include a Thai boxing ring from Bangkok, an Andalusian Osborne bull from Costa del Sol, manhole covers from Zanzibar and Tel Aviv, an eight-point star fountain from Morocco, and a public DJ sound system from Jamaica. The result is an unlikely hybrid that demystifies difference and materializes a progressive politics of pluralism. Like the conceptual starting point for *Violence of the Garden* at Métis, *Superkilen* demonstrates Topotek 1's aptitude for identifying structures of contention, using design to alter perspectives and behaviours through a creative conflation of incompatibilities. Their work is a critique of arbitrary division (whether barbed wire fence to keep out unwanted pests or visitors as at Métis, or social conventions that result in the marginalization of groups as at *Superkilen*), and aspires to create a level playing field for equality and participation.

REAFFIRMING CONCEPTUAL CONVICTIONS

One accomplished practice to reaffirm its attitude of practice at Métis is Michael Van Valkenburgh Associates (MVVA), with their 2011 garden titled *This Rocks! Get Lost!* (pages 164–169). This garden attests to their priority for boldly reconsidering the subtle elements that compose a timeless landscape. Tapping into the subconscious, their attitude of practice invokes the latent context and background of personal memory and experience through a seemingly effortless yet critical composition of archetypal features that, in their words, "unlock doors to deeper thoughts".

Their garden at Métis is a study in subtlety, made up of several large rough-quarried masses of white Vermont marble, replete with brute quarry scars and other process imperfections that give the objects an appearance that is neither fully natural nor human-made. Each block is 'randomly' placed throughout a small boreal forest clearing, the dark cool greens of existing spruce and cedar highlighted by booster planting of lighter yellow-hued Eastern white pine. These nuanced moves enhance the contrast between the matte gleam of the marble monoliths and the seemingly infinite forest backdrop, creating a strangely unfamiliar setting (Vermont marble in Gaspésie) that feels reassuringly indigenous at the same time. This study is a test of the firm's conceptual convictions which underlie their fundamental assumptions of practice.

This Rocks! Get Lost! condenses an attitude for enabling precarious juxtapositions of natural process, human aspiration, and an open-ended looseness to accommodate future unforeseen demands, all within a subtle framework that is powerful for the sum of its mutually crafted parts. The large-scale public parks by MVVA are consistent in demonstrating these same principles of practice in composing a naturalized picturesque that goes beyond mere scenery, a kind of benevolent 'Frankenstein' between human artifice and natural process.

One example is Brooklyn Bridge Park, which transforms a derelict post-industrial waterfront divorced from the urban fabric by the Brooklyn-Queens Expressway. Like an enormous green roof, this highly engineered park is built over pier structures in the East River to support a rich tapestry of undulating promenades, grassy slopes and fields, forest and bramble corridors, a constructed beach and kayak launch, discrete sports areas, and a large public gathering space. The sum of these layers results in an exaggerated urban wilderness, where the filigree of paths weave between intimate pockets that open up to sweeping views of the Manhattan skyline, a striking counterpoint and visual climax on the opposite shore.

Another example is *Teardrop Park* in Battery Park City where natural process is constructed over an underground parking structure to adapt a compact Hudson River Valley eco-system into Lower Manhattan. Similar to their quarried marble erratics at Métis, the duplicity between natural process and human craft is dissolved by a large constructed sedimentary rock anticline structure that is both cliff and wall.

Teardrop Park, New York, Michael Van Valkenburgh Associates

Teardrop Park, New York, Michael Van Valkenburgh Associates

The MVVA garden at Métis distills the essence of these two New York projects, reaffirming the conceptual premise of their practice towards a continued optimism for the plausible symbiosis between natural systems and human agency.

GRAFTING IDEAS FOR CONTINUED EXPLORATION

The gardens at Métis provide fertile ground for germinating ideas, which can then subsequently be transplanted to take root and grow in new directions someplace else. One example is the garden *Making Circles in the Water* (pages 58–61), installed at Métis in 2011 by Diana Balmori Associates. The garden emphasizes the priority in her practice to establish connections with context through a manipulation of layered frames that direct the gaze of the viewer and inform a way of seeing. Composed by a succession of progressively expanding circles towards the cliff side view of the St. Lawrence River panorama, the visitor is drawn into a direct relationship with the unbound expanse of the horizon. The rhythm of the widening circles across a succession of lighter greys and the path of reflective circular pavers build a visual momentum that traces a path for the viewer's gaze into the infinity of the maritime horizon.

At the core of Balmori's practice is an aspiration to reawaken both visual and mental perspectives though gestures that renew relationships with place. This restoration of the forgotten vista, as at the garden in Métis, underlies Balmori's subsequent explorations that aim to reactivate significant sites of neglect. One example is her 2015 experimental installation titled *GrowOnUs*, where the succession of sightlines begun at Métis continues as a physical extension off shore, this time into Brooklyn's Gowanus Canal, one of the most polluted bodies of water in the United States.

The experiment at the Gowanus Canal carries on as an agglomeration of upright zinc-coated culverts, the same ones typically used to convey pollutants into this waterway, arranged on a buoyant structure to become floating vegetated islands. Each culvert explores the viability of options for planting, phytoremediation, and irrigation. This 'cyborg' crossbreed between nature and structure aims to ultimately consider the possibility of larger-scale floating landscapes on contaminated waterways in cities where open space is in short supply. This futuristic vision aspires to create multi-functional green infrastructure that could become park, farm, biodiversity habitat, shoreline protection, or energy generator. Equally important however to the performance of these functions is the renewed perspective of this highly visible yet overlooked site, and the optimism it creates to actualize its renewed status.

CONVERGENCE AS PRACTICE

Consistent among the practices described here, and many others who have left their mark at the Métis International Garden Festival, is an approach to landscape architecture that responsibly resolves functional and technical requisites through a conceptual lens which ultimately elevates the coherent expression of a cultural idea. This convergence between work of art and practice of landscape architecture attests to the priority in the field now given to expressing an idea through the medium of landscape. This convergence between art and landscape is what has become the raison d'être for the experimental gardens at Métis. The practice of ideas cultivated at Métis is propagated through the practice of landscape architecture into the public imagination to become new perspectives, informing our understanding and affirming the place of creativity in giving shape to the commons of public life.

***GrowOnUs*, Brooklyn, New York, Balmori Associates**

LANDSCAPE AS A LIVING EXPERIENCE

The natural landscape is so present, so constant, and seemingly unchanging that we often forget to look at it as a continually shifting, evolving, and changing system.

The gardens in this chapter invite a close reading of the dynamics of their surrounding environment by immersing visitors in subtly enhanced versions of the existing landscape. These are not didactic or interpretive displays intended to simply show us how something works, they are complete experiences designed to open all of our senses to the timescales, processes, and materials that shape the environment around us.

Some of these gardens simulate or accelerate natural processes (*Histoire sans fin ou Le bois dans tous ses états, Le jardin de la connaissance*, *Afterburn*), some use the forces of the site as a design input (*Sound Field*), and others simply offer us access to a landscape where we can take the time to feel its power (*This Rocks! Get Lost!*).

Each garden plays with the tension between the natural and the anthropogenic, offering just enough hints at the latter for visitors to ask, "What is happening here?" This curiosity encourages them to focus their reading of the landscape in search of their own answers and ultimately a heightened awareness of the world around them.

HISTOIRE SANS FIN OU LE BOIS DANS TOUS SES ETATS

Atelier eem

2012–

Abstract

Histoire sans fin ou Le bois dans tous ses états subtly amplifies the evolution of a post-disturbance landscape to invite a closer reading of the ongoing story of the site.

Method

This garden stages a natural succession, but accelerates it by implanting 'time speeders' (mushrooms, mosses, and pioneer plants) to condense the process and make it more legible to visitors. This is not meant to be a didactic journey, but a careful exercise in reading the clues of the landscape.

A black slate groundcover points to a disturbance (fire, disease, disaster) that has forced the landscape to start again from zero. The following process of regeneration unfolds for the visitor as ten walls of stacked logs—each representing one stage of re-colonization—move through the cycles of a landscape as it establishes, thrives, and decays.

The walls are laid out in a progression from most recently disturbed to most established and are planted sequentially with mushrooms, transplanted mosses, perennials, grasses, and small trees to demonstrate the stages of growth as one landscape evolves to replace the one before it. Higher walls are piled with the freshest wood and become lower as they represent older landscapes. Each of the walls will eventually decay and return back to the earth.

Result

By amplifying the process of forest succession, this project immerses visitors in the experience of reading the landscape and invites them to consider the timescale of the natural and human-influence worlds.

Materials

Chopped wood (estimated 50 tons), mushrooms, mosses, seedbombs containing perennials, grasses, trees and shrubs, bryophytes harvested on site, crushed slate, geotextile

Walls of stacked logs present the forest at successive stages of evolution.

With time, grasses, mosses, seeds, and ferns begin to colonize the walls.

An estimated 50 tons of logs are stacked to form the walls.

Mushrooms
Pleurotus citrinopileatus
Pleurotus citrinus
Pleurotus djamor
Pleurotus eryngii
Pleurotus ostreotus
Lentinula edodes
Hericium ericaceus
Ganoderma lucidum
Ganoderme luisant
Hypsizigus ulmarius
Lentinula edodes
Stropharia rugosoannulata
Agrocybe aegerita
Ganoderma lucidum
Hericium erinaceus
Pietra fungaia

Mosses
Collected and transplanted on site; species undetermined

Seeds
Perennials:
Achillea millefolium 1%
Chamerion angustifolium (Epilobium angustifolium) 1%
Doellingeria umbellate 3%
Oenothera biennis 6%
Solidago Canadensis 1%
Solidago nemoralis 2%
Symphyotrichum novae-angliae 2%

Grasses
Elymus trachycaulus 17%
Festuca rubra 30%
Lolium multiflorum 11%

Trees and shrubs
Alnus incana ssp. rugosa (A. rugosa) 3%
Betula populifolia 1%
Cornus stolonifera 3%
Prunus virginiana 9%
Rhus typhina 7%
Spiraea tomentosa 1%
Spiraea alba var. latifolia 1%

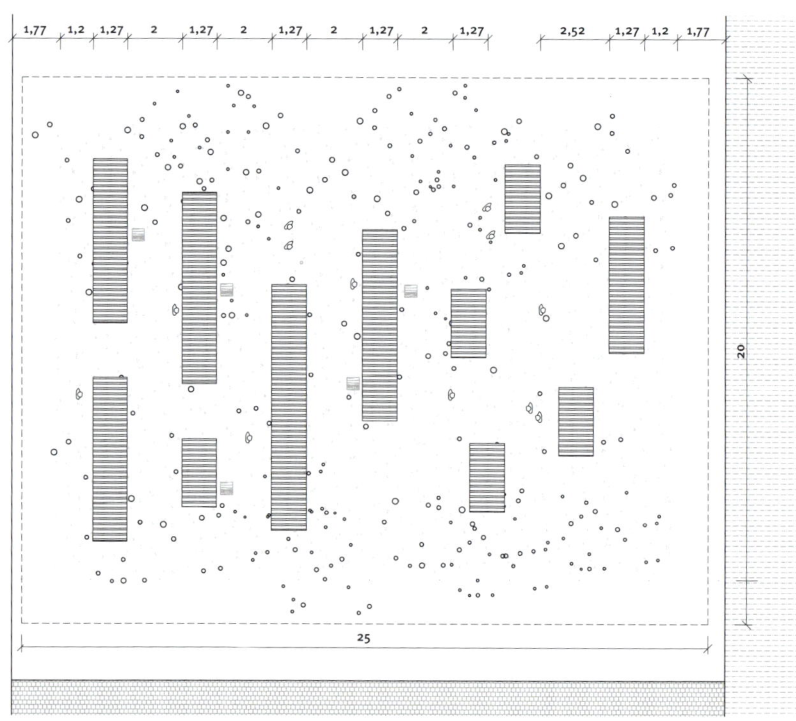

Layout plan

"When you see the forest as a timescape, you see that you always have an evolution. Even if you burn everything down, in time a new landscape will come."

Marc Blume

LE JARDIN DE LA CONNAISSANCE

100Landschaftsarchitektur + Rodney LaTourelle

2010–2013

Abstract

Le jardin de la connaissance (The Garden of Knowledge) exposes the fragile and timeless material of books to the temporality of nature to elicit emotional involvement from the visitor.

Method

This garden uses the material of knowledge to create a spatial experience of decay, seasons, and time. Forty thousand books are used to construct walls for people to touch, benches to sit on, and carpets to walk across—each designed to invite a reaction as these beautiful and valuable materials are subject to time, moisture, and decay. The process of decomposition is accelerated by planting the structures with varieties of mushrooms that grow and feed off the books as they begin to break down.

The self-supporting book walls are stabilized with brightly painted wooden boards inserted between the rows of books. The boards act not only as a physical structure, but as a time structure as well: as the books weather and fade, the colour and composition of the wood remains the same, registering the passage of time and the ongoing decay of the books.

Result

This piece evoked a strong reaction in visitors as they saw these precious carriers of knowledge dying and rotting out in the open. Some were appalled by this allocation of resources, others saddened by what they saw as the destruction of the French-language heritage they had fought so hard for, and others were delighted and amazed by this visual and emotional experience.

Materials

Approx. 40,000 books from local public and school libraries, mushrooms, painted boards

Approx. 40,000 books are exposed to the elements to elicit emotional reactions from festival visitors.

Mushrooms
Shaggy mane *(coprinus comatus)*
Oyster (yellow oyster) *(pleurotus citrinopileatus)*
Blue oyster *(pleurotus columbinus)*
Oyster (pink oyster) *(pleurotus djamor)*
Oyster (king oyster) *(pleurotus eryngii)*
(Pearl) oyster *(pleurotus ostreatus)*
(Phoenix) Indian oyster *(pleurotus pulmonarius)*
Poule de bois / maitake *(grifola frondosa)*
Wine cap *(stropharia rugoso-annulata)*

Mushrooms are planted among the books to accelerate the decomposition process.

Painted boards provide physical structure and offer a register of time as they remain vibrant while the books weather and fade.

“It was very important to us to not make a didactic garden. It was not a statement about saving the world by recycling paper. It was not about a return to nature. It was really about letting people discover the place and making their own reactions to it.”

Thilo Folkerts

AFTERBURN
Civilian Projects
2014–2015

Abstract
Afterburn gives us access to a powerful and ecologically significant landscape that we would otherwise not be able to experience.

Method
Canada's boreal forest covers almost 60 percent of the country's land area and remains healthy and diverse through forest fires, both natural and human-controlled. Despite their frequency, we do not usually get to experience these often remote post-fire landscapes—their textures, their smells, and their ecological richness—as they begin to re-establish and grow.

To reveal both the destructive traces and the regenerative potential of controlled burns, this garden re-creates a post-fire landscape with a grid of 150 charred posts. Visitors can feel the texture of the scorched wood, smell the char as it becomes stronger under direct sunlight, and see the unexpected ripple effect as the hinged wood fibres lift and fall with the winds off the St. Lawrence River. The posts are marked with orange surveyor's paint, evoking the human hand in forest management.

Visitors can experience the rebirth of the forest as pioneer conifer saplings and local perennials struggle to survive and become the next mature forest. The dichotomy of destruction and life is most keenly felt here as visitors see the contrast between the stark charred posts and the feathery, green, and vibrant pioneer species.

Result
This garden offers visitors a clearer reading of the destructive power and regenerative strength of controlled burns by providing close access to the subtle material changes and textures of these large and unfamiliar landscapes.

Materials
150 (10 x 10 x 4.85 metres) posts, conifer saplings, local perennials, gravel, marking paint

Visitors have an up-close experience with the textures, colours and smells of the charred wood.

Balsam fir (*abies balsamea*)
Larch (tamarack)(*larix laricina*)
White spruce (*picea glauca*)
Black spruce (*picea mariana*)
Jack pine (*pinus banksiana*)
Lodgepole pine (*pinus contorta*)
Calypso orchid (*calypso bulbosa*)
Fireweed (*chamerion angustifolium*)
Sheep laurel (*kalmia angustifolia*)

Pioneer conifer saplings and local perrenials begin the process of regeneration.

A field of charred posts allows visitors to experience the process of destruction and re-birth after a controlled burn.

"We were interested in the interplay between something so dead, but also so incredibly alive. We wanted people to see that it's not about barrenness, but about regeneration."

Nicko Elliot

Sheep laurel (*kalmia angustifolia*)

SOUND FIELD
Douglas Moffat and Steve Bates
2007–2009

Abstract
Sound Field works with the dynamics of its site to create a sonic composition that heightens our awareness of the surrounding landscape.

Method
Instead of simply amplifying the sounds of the site, the composition engages in a conversation with a grove of poplar trees as it chatters and roars in response to the shifting winds off the St. Lawrence River. An array of small speakers is controlled by wind sensors that dictate the intensity and fluctuation of the artificial sound in response to the intensity and fluctuation of the wind. As the sound of the poplars increases, the intensity of the artificial sound diminishes. As the wind dies down and the poplars are silenced, the artificial sound takes over. This ongoing and constantly changing conversation lasts for the duration of the festival (nearly 129,600 minutes) and, like the surrounding St. Lawrence landscape, it will never sound the same twice.

The compositional strategy for the sound also takes it cues from the local landscape. Built using a collection of small sound elements (short tones, diffuse clicks, and fractured electronic drones), it recalls the aggregate 'applauding' texture that the tiny clapping leaves of poplars make as they are agitated by the wind.

Gravel pathways and long benches offer an intimate listening area beneath the tree canopy, where attentive visitors will begin to make this connection to the larger landscape.

Result
Sound Field offers an immediate sonic experience, but encourages a longer listening as well. Once visitors get more tuned in to the relationship of the natural and artificial sounds, they will become more aware of the site and its dynamics.

Materials
Speakers, tripod bases, cables, audio amplifiers, five wind sensors (anemometers), concrete board benches, gravel, low barrier-edge for blue-poppy protection

A wind-sensitive sound composition responds to the winds off the St. Lawrence River to create a constantly changing, site-specific sonic experience.

Tripod speaker bases are designed without footings to be sensitive to Elsie Reford's famous Himalayan Blue Poppies.

Benches designed and built by Jake Moore

"We knew that we already had a fantastic-sounding natural landscape, so we wanted to find a way to weave something into it that encouraged you to listen to what was already there."

Douglas Moffat

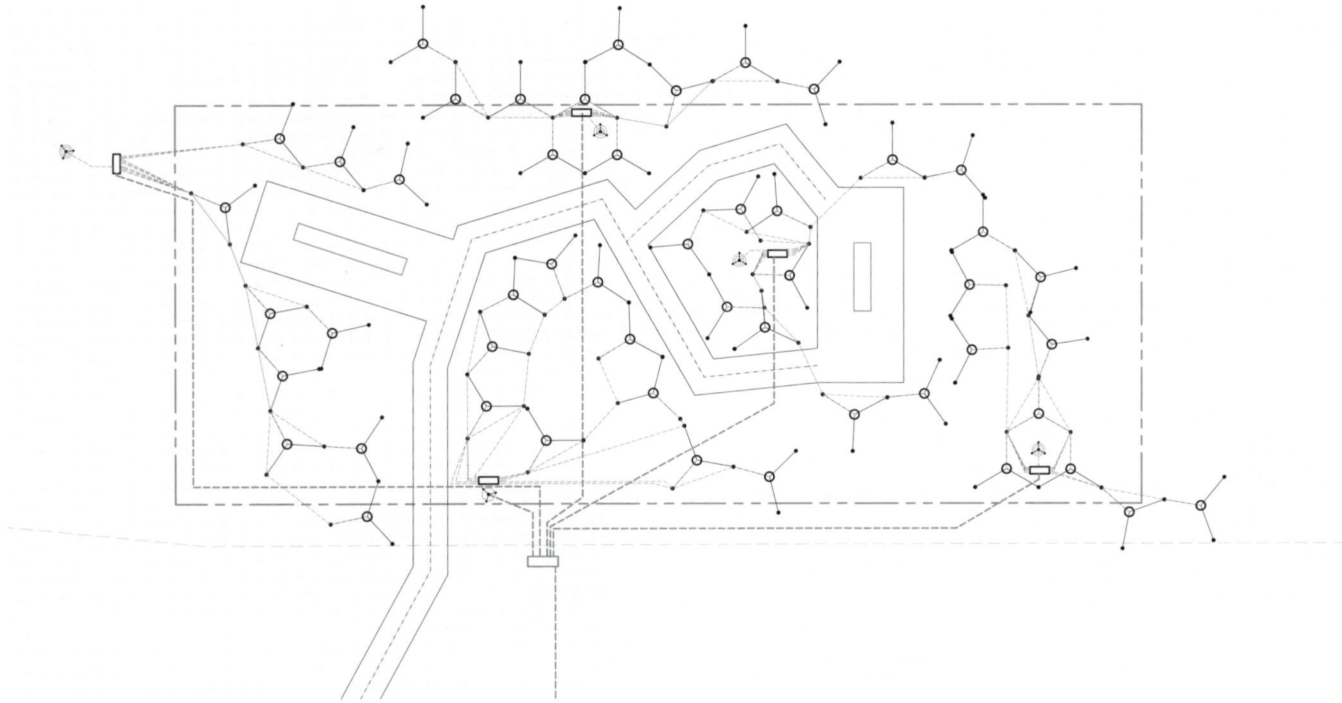

Wiring plan

All weather electronics designed by BASH / Geoffrey Jones

THIS ROCKS! GET LOST!
Michael Van Valkenburgh Associates
2011–

Abstract
This Rocks! Get Lost! evokes a deep visceral reaction by engulfing visitors in a world of raw landscape materials.

Method
This garden stages an encounter with five huge chunks of raw Vermont marble, a material we most often experience as polished café table tops and bathroom tiles. The impressive, weighty rocks (up to 1.85 x 2.6 metres) are clearly from the earth with their irregular shapes, rough surfaces, and surprising range of colours and vein patterns. Only the spray-painted identification tags from the quarry and the curious grooved surfaces give any hint at their provenance.

The garden is laid out to draw visitors into a choreographed experience with these powerful raw materials. As people move through a series of spaces and niches between the rocks, they are forced to navigate around the volumes, to understand them, and to consider their materiality. This naturally occurring stone feels just enough out of place (and scale) on this boreal forest site that visitors may pause to wonder, "How did this get here?" As the title suggests, people are invited to 'get lost' in this landscape experience.

Result
By physically engaging visitors with a sense of tactility and rawness, this garden offers us a moment to remember that landscape has the power to evoke emotions, to transport us, or even to unlock doors within our deepest thoughts.

Materials
Vermont marble, white pine (*Pinus strobus*), arborvitae (*Thuja occidentalis*), pine needles

Five chunks of raw Vermont marble engulf visitors in a felt landscape experience.

Marble off-cuts with varying colours and patterns are specifically selected for the garden.

"I wanted to do a project where the power of landscape material was the whole idea."

Michael Van Valkenburgh

APPENDIX

MÉTIS INTERNATIONAL GARDEN FESTIVAL 2000–2016

2000

Jill Billington, United Kingdom
Clearings
2000

Claude Cormier + Associés, Canada
Blue Stick Garden
2000

Espace drar (Patricia Lussier, Anna Radice), Canada
Not in My Backyard
2000–2001

Susan Herrington, Canada
Surf and Turf
2000

Marie-Christine Landry, Canada
Le jardin des appels
2000

Jennifer Luce, United States
Transfusion
2000

PLANT (Christopher Pommer, Lisa Rapoport, Mary Tremain), Canada
Le jardin du repos
2000

Bernard Saint-Denis, Peter Fianu, Canada
Living Room
2000

2001

Atelier Pierre Thibault (with Katherine McKinnon, Vadim Siegel), Canada
Jardin territoire
2001

Sophie Beaudoin, Marie-Ève Cardinal, Michèle Gauthier, Canada
Sous la pelouse, le jardin
2001

BGL (Jasmin Bilodeau, Sébastien Giguère, Nicolas Laverdière), Canada
Sentier battu
2001

Michel Boulcourt, France
Une semaine au potager
2001

Dominique Caire, France
Couleurs du temps
2001

Bernard Lassus, France
Être là un peu...+
2001

NIPpaysage (Mathieu Casavant, France Cormier, Josée Labelle, Michel Langevin, Mélanie Mignault), Canada *In vitro*
2001

Research & Development in Architecture (Richard Davignon, Laura Plosz, Troy Smith), Canada
Narcissist Narcoses
2001

2002

Atelier Big City (Randy Cohen, Anne Cormier, Howard Davies), Canada
Garden Party
2002

Christopher Bradley-Hole, United Kingdom
Layers
2002

Bonita Bulaitis, United Kingdom
No Strings Attached
2002

Paul Cooper, United Kingdom
The Eden Laboratory
2002

LAND-I (Marco Antonini, Roberto Capecci, Raffaella Sini), Italy
Ombre
2002

Marie Claude Massicotte, Raquel Peñalosa (with Gustavo Ramirez Nieto, Lise Rivest), Canada
A Garden Is Never Finished
2002

Chris Matthews, Taco Iwashima, United States
You Are Here Garden
2002–2003

Mousse Architecture de paysage (Charlotte Gaudette, Emmanuelle Tittley), Canada
Catimini
2002

2003

Siham Ben Sari, Morocco
O Hendiya
2003

Marc Böhlen, Natalie Tan, Canada
Unseen
2003

EKIP (Thierry Beaudoin, Sinisha Brdar, Patrick Morand, Marc Pape), Canada
Parallaxe Boogie-Woogie
2003–2004

Maria Goula, Anna Zahonero (with Alexandre Campello, Andrew Harris, Claudia Illanes), Spain
Summer-dry
2003

Hal Ingberg, Canada
Réflexions colorées
2003–

Antonio Perazzi, Italy
Bleu de bois
2003–2004

SE BUSCA / WANTED (Michele Adrian, Paula Meijerink), United States
Asphalt Garden
2003

Studio.eu (Paola Cannavò, Ippolita Nicotera, Francesca Venier), Italy
Italian Fragment
2003

Stefan Tischer, Canada
Homme-Nature-Jardin
2003

2004

Atelier Big City (Randy Cohen, Anne Cormier, Howard Davies), Canada
Head in the Clouds
2004–2005

Pierre Bélanger, Canada
Macroscope
2004

BGL (Jasmin Bilodeau, Sébastien Giguère, Nicolas Laverdière), Canada
La source
2004–2005

Susan Herrington, Canada
Hip Hop
2004–2005

Mousse Architecture de paysage (Charlotte Gaudette, Emmanuelle Tittley), Canada
Mobile Landscape Intervention Unit
2004–2005

SE BUSCA / WANTED (Michele Adrian, Paula Meijerink), United States
Shushu
2004

2005

AMMA architecture de paysage (Amélie Germain, Marie-Andrée Huard), Canada
Nettoyage à sec
2005

Aranda\Lasch (Benjamin Aranda, Chris Lasch), United States
Camouflage View
2005–2007

Pierre Bourgault, Maxime Bourgault, Canada
Un jardin en mer
2005

Philippe Coignet, David Serero, France
Modulations
2005–2006

Glenn Herman, Charles Waldheim (with Jessie Peterman, Shannon Lee), Canada
Subterranean
2005

Lateral Architecture (Lola Sheppard, Mason White), Canada
Soil Horizon
2005

Taylor Cullity Lethlean (Kate Cullity with Ryan Sims), Australia
Eucalyptus – Light and Shadow
2005

2006

AMMA architecture de paysage (Amélie Germain, Marie-Andrée Huard), Canada
Nettoyage à sec II : Tomber dans la lune
2006

atelier le balto (Véronique Faucheur, Marc Pouzol, Marc Vatinel), France and Germany
Bois de biais: Ces jours-ci je suis fier de mon petit paradis
2006–2009

Bosses design (Éric Daoust, Donald Potvin, Jean-François Potvin), Canada
L'effet des serres
2006

CAO PERROT (Andy Cao, Xavier Perrot), United States and France
Le jardin des Hespérides
2006–2007

Cédule 40 (Julien Boily, Sonia Boudreau, Étienne Boulanger, Noémie Payant-Hébert), Canada
Sous-terrain de jeu
2006

North Design Office (Peter North, Alissa North), Canada
Core Sample
2006–2008

Stoss Landscape Urbanism (Chris Reed, Chris Muskopf, Scott Bishop, Kristin Malone), United States
Safe Zone
2006–2009

Taylor Cullity Lethlean (Kate Cullity with Ryan Sims), Australia
Eucalyptus Lost
2006

2007

Bosses design (Éric Daoust, Donald Potvin, Jean-François Potvin), Canada
L'effet desért
2007

Catalyse urbaine (Juliette Patterson, Michel Langlois, Gerard Leckey), Canada
Cat's Cradle
2007

Cédule 40 (Julien Boily, Sonia Boudreau, Étienne Boulanger, Noémie Payant-Hébert), Canada
Terrain fertile
2007

Jasmin Corbeil, Stéphane Bertrand, Jean-Maxime Dufresne, Canada
La boîte noire
2007–2008

Angela Iarocci, Claire Ironside, David Ross, Canada
Pomme de parterre
2007–2010

Douglas Moffat and Steve Bates, Canada
Sound Field
2007–2009

2008

À 4 (Claudia Delisle, Karine Dieujuste, Philippe Nolet, Sami Tannoury), Canada
Poule mouillée
2008–2009

Federico Brancalion, Francesca Moretti, Mirando Di Prinzo, Rodolfo Roncella, Italy
Réflexions suspendues – Sospese riflessioni
2008–2010

Cédule 40 (Julien Boily, Sonia Boudreau, Étienne Boulanger, Noémie Payant-Hébert), Canada
Les ondées aratoires
2008

Legge Lewis Legge (Andrea Legge, Deborah Lewis, Murray Legge), Canada and United States
Round Up (d'après Monet)
2008–2009

NIPpaysage (Mathieu Casavant, France Cormier, Josée Labelle, Michel Langevin, Mélanie Mignault), Canada
Bon arbre au bon endroit
2008–2012

Rita (Karine Corbeil, Stéphane Rita Halmaï-Voisard, Francis Rollin), Canada
Passe-moi un sapin Rita
2008–2009

2009

Jane Hutton, Adrian Blackwell, Canada
Dymaxion Sleep (curled up)
2009–2013

Legge Lewis Legge (Andrea Legge, Deborah Lewis, Murray Legge), Canada and United States
Fractal Garden
2009–2013

Deborah Nagan, United Kingdom
Every Garden Needs a Shed and a Lawn!
2009–2013

Suresh Perera, Canada
forest.SQUARE.sky.
2009–2010

Mateo Pinto, Carolina Cisneros, Victoria Marshall, United States
Seedling
2009–2010

spmb (Eduardo Aquino, Karen Shanski) with Ralph Glor, Matt Baker, Martin Gagnon, Canada
HAHA!
2009–2014

Craig Verzone, Christina Woods, Dragos Ivanet, Switzerland
Hayground
2009

2010

atelier le balto (Véronique Faucheur, Marc Pouzol, Marc Vatinel), France and Germany
Bois de biais: Ces jours-ci je suis fier de mon petit
2010

Claude Cormier + Associés, Canada
Blue Stick Garden
2010–2012

Rosetta Elkin, Canada
Tiny Taxonomy
2010–

Habitation (David Vago, Simone Marsh, Nick Brown), Australia
The Grass Is Greener
2010

Legge Lewis Legge (Andrea Legge, Deborah Lewis, Murray Legge), Canada and United States
Double Serpent
2010

NIPpaysage (Mathieu Casavant, France Cormier, Josée Labelle, Michel Langevin, Mélanie Mignault), Canada
Oursins
2010–2012

relais Landschaftsarchitekten (Gero Heck, Marianne Mommsen), Germany
Tree Stands
2010–2012

Studio Bryan Hanes (Bryan Hanes, Jose Menendez, Yadiel Rivera Diaz, Brenna Herpmann) and DIGSAU (Jules Dingle, Jeff Goldstein, Mark Sanderson, Jamie Unkefer, Aaron Jezzi), United States
Veil Garden
2010–

Topotek 1 (Martin Rein-Cano, Lorenz Dexler), Germany
Violence of the Garden (Land Use Observatory)
2010–2012

100Landschaftsarchitektur (Thilo Folkerts) and Rodney LaTourelle, Germany and Canada
Le jardin de la connaissance
2010–2013

2011

asensio_mah (Leire Asensio-Villoria, David Mah) and students from the Graduate School of Design, Harvard University, United States
Surface Deep
2011–2014

atelier le balto (Véronique Faucheur, Marc Pouzol, Marc Vatinel) and Kai Schiemenz, France and Germany
Bois de biais et sa folie
2011–

Balmori Associates (Diana Balmori, Noémie Lafaurie-Debany, Isabelle Desfoux, Sarah Falbe-Hansen, Patricio Fernandez), United States
Making Circles in the Water
2011–

Habitation (David Vago, Simone Marsh, Nick Brown), Australia
The Grass Is Greener (Mirror mirror on the floor what's beyond the great grass wall)
2011

Heather Ring, Brenda Parker, Synnøve Fredericks, United Kingdom
Algaegarden
2011–2013

North Design Office (Peter North, Alissa North), Canada
Itinerant Pods
2011–2013

Ken Smith, United States
A Ditch With A View
2011–

Terragram (Vladimir Sitta, Anita Madura, Robert Faber), Australia
Noli Tangere
2011–2012

Topotek 1 (Martin Rein-Cano, Lorenz Dexler), Germany
Land Use Observatory (Sound and Internet Installation)
2011–2012

Urbanbees (Marco Asciutti, Farzaneh Bahrami, Enrique Enriquez, Matteo Muggianu), Canada, Italy, and Switzerland
Fleur de sel
2011

Michael Van Valkenburgh Associates, United States
This Rocks! Get Lost!
2011–

2012

Atelier eem (Marc Blume, Francesca Liggieri, Estelle Nicod, Héloïse Blanzat), France
Histoire sans fin ou Le bois dans tous ses états
2012–

ATLAS (Kimberly Garza, Andrew ten Brink) and Forbes Lipschitz, United States
15 KNOTS
2012–2013

Laura B. Garófalo, United States
Buoyant
2012–2013

Les attentives (Chloé B. Fortin, Audrey Lavallée), Canada
La collection du jardinier
2012–2014

Ekachai Pattamasattayasonthi and dL STUDIO (Tom Lee, Soren deNiord), United States
Garden=Folly
2012

2013

Atelier Barda (Patrick Morand, Antonio Di Bacco, Cécile Combelle, Julien Pinard), Canada
Sacré potager
2013–2015

Nicholas Croft, Michaela MacLeod, United States and Canada
Pink Punch
2013–2014

Ecoid (Yongkyu Kim, Jonghyun Baek), United States
Smart Small
2013

NIPpaysage (Mathieu Casavant, Josée Labelle, Michel Langevin, Mélanie Mignault, France Cormier, Émilie Bertrand-Villemure, Claude Cournoyer, Sylvain Lenoir, Johanna Ballhaus, Benjamin Deshaies, Mélanie Pelchat, Catherine Blain), Canada
Bon arbre au bon endroit « Souvenir d'enfance »
2013–

Johan Selbing, Anouk Vogel, Netherlands
Courtesy of Nature
2013–

Snøhetta (Claire Fellman, Nick Koster, Karli Molter, Misako Murata, Maura Rockcastle), United States and Norway
Edge Effect
2013–

Carlos M. Teixeira, Brazil
Dead Garden II
2013–

2014

Atelier Pierre Thibault, Canada
Jardins M
2014–

Châssi (Caroline Magar, Marie-Josée Gagnon, François Leblanc), Canada
Méristème
2014–2015

CITYLABORATORY (Aurora Armental Ruiz, Stefano Ciurlo Walker), Spain
Rotunda
2014–

Civilian Projects (Ksenia Kagner, Nicko Elliott), Canada and United States
Afterburn
2014–2015

Julia Jamrozik, Coryn Kempster, Canada and Switzerland
Line Garden
2014

Livescape (Seungjong Yoo, Byoungjoon Kim, Hyeryoung Cho, Yongchul Cho, Iltae Jeong, Jinhwan Kim, Soojung Yoon), South Korea
Cone Garden
2014–2015

Nomad Studio (William E. Roberts, Laura Santín), United States
Orange Secret
2014–

Annie Ypperciel, Robert Desjardins, Canada
Bal à la villa
2014–2015

2015

Ophélie Bouvet, Kihan Kim, France
Carré bleu sur fond blanc
2015–

Groupe A / Annexe U (Jean-François Laroche, Rémi Morency, Erick Rivard, Maxime Rousseau), Canada
Se mouiller (la belle échappée)
2015

Meaghan Hunter, Suzy Melo, Canada
Popple
2015

Talmon Biran architecture studio (Roy Talmon, Noa Biran), Israel
Around-About
2015–

University of Toronto (Peter North with students Jordan Duke, Jasper Flores, Dayne Roy-Caldwell, Anna Rosen, Nicholas Gosselin, Hanna Chung, Jaclyn Ryback, Siqi Li, Ameneh Kadivar, Tamar Pister, Yingyi Zhao, Anita Manitius), Canada
Macro/Micro/Myco
2015–

1986 architecture (Mathilde Gaudemet, Arthur Ozenne), France
I Like to Move It
2015–

2016

Romy Brosseau, Rosemarie Faille-Faubert, Émilie Gagné-Loranger, Canada
La maison de Jacques
2016

Craig Chapple, United States
Cyclops
2016

Coache Lacaille paysagistes (Maxime Coache, Victor Lacaille, Luc Dallanora), France
Carbone
2016

Ran Hwang, Sangmok Kim, Sungwoo Kim, Shin Hee Park, South Korea, China, and United States
Dress Up!
2016

Christian Poules, Switzerland
Le caveau
2016

SRCW (Sean Radford, Chris Wiebe), Canada
TiiLT
2016

EXTRA-MUROS
OFF-SITE INSTALLATIONS

2003

Atelier Pierre Thibault , Canada
Les jardins mobiles
New Richmond, Québec, Canada
2003

Claude Cormier + Associés, Canada
Solange
Domaine de Lacroix-Laval, Lyon, France
2003

Espace drar (Patricia Lussier, Anna Radice), Canada
À propos du blanc
Amqui, Québec, Canada
2003

Mousse Architecture de paysage (Charlotte Gaudette, Emmanuelle Tittley), Canada
Éruption
Montréal, Québec, Canada
2003

NIPpaysage (Mathieu Casavant, France Cormier, Josée Labelle, Michel Langevin, Mélanie Mignault), Canada
Flore laurentienne
Ortus Artis, San Lorenzo de Padula, Italy
2003

2004

Claude Cormier + Associés, Canada
Blue Stick Garden
Hestercombe Gardens, United Kingdom
2004

2005

NIPpaysage (Mathieu Casavant, France Cormier, Josée Labelle, Michel Langevin, Mélanie Mignault), Canada
Une mer d'idées
Canada Blooms, Toronto, Canada
2005

2006

Atelier in situ (Annie Lebel, Stéphane Pratte), Canada
10 000 UP
Victoria Square, Montréal, Canada
2006

Claude Cormier + Associés, Canada
Blue Stick Garden
International Flora Montréal, Montréal, Canada
2006

Mousse Architecture de paysage (Charlotte Gaudette, Emmanuelle Tittley), Canada
Mobile Landscape Intervention Unit
Brick Works, Toronto, Canada
2006

2009

NIPpaysage (Mathieu Casavant, France Cormier, Josée Labelle, Michel Langevin, Mélanie Mignault), Canada
Oursins
Métis-sur-Montréal (Place De La Dauversière), Canada
2009

Rita (Karine Corbeil, Stéphane Halmaï-Voisard), Canada
Venez-jouer dans nos plates-bandes/Come Play in Our Garden
Canada Blooms, Toronto, Canada
2009

2010

NIPpaysage (Mathieu Casavant, France Cormier, Josée Labelle, Michel Langevin, Mélanie Mignault), Canada
Oursins
Canada Blooms, Toronto, Canada
2010

Philippe Nolet, Canada
Broderie buchée
Métis-sur-Montréal (Place De La Dauversière), Canada
2010

Rita (Karine Corbeil, Stéphane Halmaï-Voisard), Canada
Passe-moi un sapin Rita/Come Play in My Garden
Métis-sur-Calgary (Celebration Gardens, Calgary), Canada
2010

2011

Deborah Nagan, United Kingdom
Every Garden Needs a Shed and a Lawn!
Canada Blooms, Toronto, Canada
2011

Heather Ring, Brenda Parker, Synnøve Fredericks, United Kingdom
Algaegarden
IIDEX Neocon, Toronto, Canada
2011

Rita (Karine Corbeil, Stéphane Halmaï-Voisard), Canada
Le sapin est un arbre
Métis-sur-Montréal (Place De La Dauversière), Canada
2011

2012

asensio_mah (Leire Asensio-Villoria, David Mah) and the Graduate School of Design, Harvard University, United States
Surface Deep
Canada Blooms, Toronto, Canada
2012

Cédule 40 (Julien Boily, Sonia Boudreau, Étienne Boulanger, Noémie Payant-Hébert), Canada
Bascule
Métis-sur-Mont-Joli, Canada
2012–2016

NIPpaysage (Mathieu Casavant, Josée Labelle, Michel Langevin, Mélanie Mignault, Claude Cournoyer, Émilie Bertrand-Villemure, Sylvain Lenoir, Johanna Ballhaus, Benjamin Deshaies), Canada
Floating Forest
Chelsea Fringe Festival, London, United Kingdom
2012

PLUX.5 (Étienne Bernier, Olivier Bourgeois, Marianne Charbonneau, Jean-Bruno Morissette, Jean-Philippe Saucier), Canada
Tisse Métis Égal
Métis-sur-Montréal (Place De La Dauversière), Canada
2012

2013

Atelier Pierre Thibault, Canada
Jardins M
Métis-sur-Montréal (Place De La Dauversière), Canada
2013

Deborah Nagan, United Kingdom
Souvent me souviens (Often Remembered)
Métis-sur-Sainte-Flavie, Canada
2013–2016

2014

Rosetta Elkin, Canada
Tiny Taxonomy
Chelsea Fringe Festival, London, United Kingdom
2014

North Design Office (Peter North, Alissa North), Canada
Itinerant Pods
Métis-sur-Montréal (Place De La Dauversière), Canada
2014

2015

École cantonale d'art de Lausanne ECAL, Switzerland
Les moutondeuses
Métis-sur-Montréal (Place De La Dauversière), Canada
2015

2000
Le jardin du repos

2001
Canada In vitro

2002
You Are Here Garden

2003
Asphalt Garden

2004
Macroscope

2005
Soil Horizon

2006
Bois de biais: Ces jours-ci je suis fier de mon petit paradis

2007
Sous-terrain de jeu

2008
Réflexions suspendues

2009
HAHA!

2010
Veil Garden

2011
The Grass Is Greener

2012
15 KNOTS

2013
Pink Punch

2014
Jardins M

2015
Popple

2016
Carbone

ACKNOWLEDGEMENTS

The authors would like to thank the following people, without whom this book would not have been possible:

Our contributors, Andy Cao and Xavier Perrot, Marc Hallé, Paula Meijerink, Alissa North, Chris Reed, Tim Richardson, and Ken Smith for generously sharing your writing and your personal reflections with us.

The festival designers for your inspiring and beautiful experiments and for taking the time to share your insights with us.

The photographers who have captured the life and character of the gardens.

Our editors at Birkhäuser, Henriette Mueller-Stahl and Ria Stein, and our graphic designer, Vera Pechel, for working with us to capture the spirit of Métis in these pages.

Jane Hutton for your many contributions to this book including your work, your support, and your critical eye.

Sylvain Legris and Marjelaine Sylvestre in the offices of Les Jardins de Métis for your editorial assistance and for meticulously going through the more than 80,000 photos to choose a handful for this book.

The Board of Directors of the Métis International Garden Festival, Pierre Bélanger, Julie Boivin, Paula Meijerink, Franck Michel, and Alexander Reford, who have been supportive of this project since its inception.

This project is supported by grants from the Conseil des arts et des lettres du Québec and the Landscape Architecture Canada Foundation. The Métis International Garden Festival is supported by the Canada Council for the Arts, Canadian Heritage, the Conseil des arts et des lettres du Québec, Emploi Québec, Tourisme Québec, and many sponsors, donors, and individual supporters.

ABOUT THE CONTRIBUTORS

Alexander Reford is the director of Les Jardins de Métis (Reford Gardens) and of the International Garden Festival. The great-grandson of Elsie Reford, he has led the restoration and transformation of her gardens since 1995. He co-founded the International Garden Festival in 2000 and has been its director since 2004. Educated at the University of Toronto and Oxford University, he is the author of articles and books on Canadian history. His books on the gardens include *Elsie's Paradise: The Reford Gardens* (2004) and its sequel on the gardens' plant collections, *Treasures of Reford Gardens: Elsie's Floral Legacy* (2006).

Emily Waugh is principal of Survey Studio, a multi-disciplinary practice focused on design communication through research, writing, exhibition design, publications, and graphic narratives. Emily has lectured in landscape architecture at the Harvard University Graduate School of Design, and the Faculty of Architecture, Landscape, and Design at the University of Toronto. Recent publications include: *Recycling Spaces: The Work of Martha Schwartz Partners* (2011); Editor, *Harvard Design Magazine* no 36. *Landscape Architecture's Core* (2013); Editor, *GSD Platform 3* (2010); and *Visionary Cities* with Winy Maas and Alexander Sverdlov (2010).

Marc Hallé is a senior associate at Claude Cormier + Associés, and lecturer in landscape architecture at the McGill University School of Architecture in Montréal. Trained in both civil engineering and landscape architecture, with an MLA from the University of Toronto, Marc's technical and artistic backgrounds combine to guide projects across the leap from pure idea to material execution, with an emphasis on sustaining their conceptual integrity throughout. Marc's previous project experience includes Evergreen Brickworks, Sugar Beach, and Berczy Park.

Tim Richardson is a garden historian and landscape critic, and the author of numerous books including *Avant Gardeners* (2009), *Futurescapes* (2011) and *Landscape and Garden Design Sketchbooks* (2015). He is a regular columnist in the *Daily Telegraph,* London, and contributes articles to the *Financial Times*, *New York Times*, *House and Garden*, *Gardens Illustrated,* and others. He wrote the landscape history course for Oxford University and in 2014–15 was visiting professor of landscape art at the University of Applied Arts Vienna (*Die Angewandte*). Tim is also founder-director of the international Chelsea Fringe Festival (2012–).

ILLUSTRATION CREDITS

All rights reserved **102** top left, top right
Aranda\Lasch **137**
asensio_mah **125** top left, **125** bottom left
Atelier Barda **133** top
Iwan Baan **140**
Balmori Associates **60** bottom, **145**
Robert Baronet **30** top, **49** bottom, **51** middle, **61** top, **75** top, **85** left, **88**, **90**, **92**, **94** top left, **117** top, **121**, **125** bottom right, **126**, **128** bottom, **129**, **155** top left, **179** top right, **180** top left
Nicola Betts **139** top
Ivan Binet **106** middle left
Adrian Blackwell **95**
Martin Bond **21**, **38**, **40** bottom, **41** top, **51** bottom, **60** top left, **64** top, **68** bottom, **70** top, **71**, **85** bottom, **98** top, **99** middle, **121** top, **133** bottom, **149**, **151** bottom right, **159** top, **167** bottom right, **180** 2nd row right, 4th row right
Suzanne Campeau **124**
Craig Chapple **111**
J. Charbonneau **154** top
Chelsea Fringe **103**
Claude Cormier + Associés **139** bottom
Coache Lacaille Paysagistes **180** bottom right
Mathieu Côté **49** top
Claude Diaz **102** bottom
Rosetta Elkin **31** middle
Festival international de jardins, Jardins de Métis/Reford Gardens **180** top right
Thilo Folkerts **154**, **155** middle, bottom
Chloé B. Fortin **41** bottom
Marc Hallé **106** middle right
Marie-Claude Hamel **25** top, **105** left
Jean-Claude Hurni **89** bottom left, **106** top, **150** top left
Hal Ingberg **74** bottom, **75** bottom left
Maïté Beauchemin Kirallah **17**
Michel Langevin **43**, **44**
Rodney LaTourelle **152**
Michel Laverdière **18**, **46**, **109** top, **114**, **117** bottom right, **160**, **162** bottom, **163**, **179** top left, 2nd left, 3rd left
Sylvain Legris **105** right, **156**
Denis Lemieux **179** 4th row left
Les Amis des Jardins de Métis Collection **104** top
Les Amis des Jardins de Métis Collection/ Robert W. Reford **14**
Yvan Maltais **81**, **104** bottom, **109** bottom left
Martha Schwartz Partners **100**, **136**
Robert Matthews **64** bottom
Michael Van Valkenburgh Associates **143**, **166**, **168**
Karli Molter **65** bottom
Anne-Renée Mongeon **57** right, **89** bottom right, **154** middle
Jeroen Musch cover image, **66**, **68** top, **69**
Paquebot Design **75** bottom right
Retis on Flickr **134**
Alexandre Rivet **80** top right
Linda Rutenberg **179** 3rd row right
Louise Tanguay **28**, **30** bottom, **31** top, bottom, **32**, **34**, **35**, **36**, **37**, **40** top, **49** middle, **50**, **51** top, **54**, **56** top, **57** left, **58**, **60** top right, bottom, **61** bottom, **62**, **70** bottom, **72**, **74** middle, **78**, **82**, **84**, **85** top right, **86**, **89** top left, right, **93**, **94** middle, bottom left, **96**, **98** bottom, **99** bottom, **104** middle, **106** bottom, **109** bottom right, **116**, **117** bottom left, **118**, **120**, **121** bottom right, **122**, **128** top left, right, **130**, **132**, **150** right, **151** top, bottom left, **162** top, **165**, **167** top left, top right, **179** 2nd row right, 4th row right, **180** 2nd row left, 3rd row left, 4th row left, 3rd row right
Gisèle Teyssier **158**, **159** bottom
Albert Vecerka/ESTO **22**
Susan Woodfine **25** bottom